Hiring Professionals
under NAFTA

Hiring Professionals under NAFTA

David Etherington
and Donna Lea Hawley

QUORUM BOOKS
Westport, Connecticut · London

Library of Congress Cataloging-in-Publication Data

Etherington, David, 1957–
    Hiring professionals under NAFTA / David B. Etherington, Donna Lea
Hawley.
        p.   cm.
    Includes bibliographical references and index.
    ISBN 1–56720–130–X (alk. paper)
        1. Alien labor, Mexican—Legal status, laws, etc.—United States.
    2. Alien labor, Canadian—Legal status, laws, etc.—United States.
    3. Professions—Law and legislation—United States.   4. Free trade—
    North America.   I. Hawley, Donna Lea.   II. Title.
    KF4829.E88   1998
    344.7301'6271—dc21   97–32988

British Library Cataloguing in Publication Data is available.

Library of Congress Catalog Card Number: 97–32988
ISBN: 1–56720–130–X

First published in 1998

Quorum Books, 88 Post Road West, Westport, CT 06881
An imprint of Greenwood Publishing Group, Inc.

Printed in the United States of America

The paper used in this book complies with the
Permanent Paper Standard issued by the National
Information Standards Organization (Z39.48–1984).

10 9 8 7 6 5 4 3 2 1

To

The Homestead at Micanopy, Florida

Contents

Preface   ix

Abbreviations   xi

I. Introduction   1

1. Introduction   3

II. Business Persons under NAFTA   11

2. Business Visitors   13

3. Treaty Traders and Treaty Investors   22

4. Intracompany Transferees   38

III. Professionals   51

5. Categories of Professionals Permitted under NAFTA   53

6. Procedures for Admission to the United States   83

7. Extension of Stay   92

8. Changing or Adding Employers   101

9. Changing and Ending Employment   112

10. Professional's Spouse and Unmarried Minor Children   115

IV. Supplementary Issues   123

11. Effect of a Strike   125

12. Changing the NAFTA Employee's Status to Permanent
    Resident   128

13. Employer Obligations for Employment Eligibility   139

Appendixes   147

A. North American Free Trade Agreement, Chapter Sixteen,
   Temporary Entry for Business Persons   149

B. North American Free Trade Agreement Implementation Act
   (Pub. L. 103-182, 107 Stat. 2057, December 8, 1993)   161

C. Immigration and Naturalization Act   164

D. Section 307, The United States–Canada Free-Trade
   Agreement Implementation Act of 1988 (Pub. L. 100-449,
   102 Stat. 1876, September 28, 1988)   166

E. Documents Recommended to Support a Petition for L-1
   Intracompany Transferee   167

F. List of INS Service Center Addresses   171

G. Translation of Documents into English   173

H. Credential Evaluation   174

I. Information Required by the Employer to Complete INS
   Form I-129   176

J. INS Forms   178

Glossary   189
References   191
Index   193

Preface

Since the signing of the North American Free Trade Agreement (NAFTA), and during the years leading up to the signing of this treaty, volumes of literature have been written about it. The value of NAFTA and of free trade has been widely debated in academic, political, and economic environments. Though much information is available about the trade provisions of NAFTA, very little has been written about its provisions concerning the international transfer of labor. For multinational business entities to remain competitive in the world market, they need to have access to international markets, not only for their products, but also for the labor force to support their multinational activities.

Though only Canada, the United States, and Mexico are parties to NAFTA, it is anticipated that one day there will be a similar treaty encompassing all of North America, Central America, South America, and the Caribbean. As this evolves, employers will increasingly be faced with the need to hire business personnel from treaty member countries.

Though NAFTA provides for the international transfer of labor, compliance with the regulations can be extremely complex and filled with traps for the unsuspecting and those that do not operate in this area on a regular and ongoing basis. In hiring non-residents, the employer will have to navigate through the ever-increasing volumes of regulations of the Immigration and Naturalization Service (INS), the Department of State, and the Department of Labor (DOL). This book attempts to provide a road map to the options available for U.S. employers in the hiring of business personnel from Mexico and Canada under NAFTA.

It has also been designed to provide the basic steps that a business owner or executive who wants to hire an employee under NAFTA can follow.

The authors have attempted to set out all of the steps that must be taken to hire such an employee. For anyone who has not completed INS forms, gathered documentation to support petitions, or completed all the steps in a petition, this book will give the basic procedures, steps, and requirements but cannot give every fine detail that may be required for every variation that presents itself in real business life. The authors have repeated descriptions on how to complete certain forms or prepare petitions. This was done so anyone using the book as a guide to completing documentation could look just at the one section explaining the specific procedure, rather than having to flip back to "see section on Mexican citizen petitions" or "see section on extensions."

Part I provides a general overview of the basic principles and requirements for bringing in temporary workers to the United States. These non-immigration principles are the basis of all entries under NAFTA. Part II examines the three business person categories permitted entry under NAFTA: business visitors, treaty traders and investors, and multinational executives. Part III, the focus of the book, discusses how American businesses can bring professionals in from Canada and Mexico as temporary employees. Part IV discusses three areas of general importance: the effect of a strike on hiring foreign employees, how to change a foreign employee's status to that of a permanent resident, and employer obligations for the employment of foreign employees.

NAFTA has been in operation for a number of years now. The INS regulations dealing with the immigration provisions of NAFTA have been set, and for the most part, don't change. However, the reader is cautioned that the law (both the statute and regulations) constantly changes. Readers should use this book as a guide only. The law may change. A small procedure, such as the inclusion of a particular document, may change. Readers need to always make a reference to the current law before completing and filing any application or petition with the INS.

Abbreviations

AILA	American Immigration Lawyers Association
CFR	Code of Federal Regulations
DOT	Dictionary of Occupational Titles of the Department of Labor
EEOC	Equal Employment Opportunity Commission
FAM	Foreign Affairs Manual
FTA	United States–Canada Free Trade Agreement
I-94	Departure document issued to temporary visitors
IIRAIRA	Illegal Immigration Reform and Immigrant Responsibility Act, 1996
IMMACT90	Immigration Act of 1990
INA	Immigration and Nationality Act
INS	Immigration and Naturalization Services
IRS	Internal Revenue Service
LCA	Labor Condition Application
NAFTA	North American Free Trade Agreement
OI	Operation Instructions (of the INS)
OOH	Occupational Outlook Handbook of the Department of Labor
POE	Port of Entry
TD	Trade Dependent

TC   Trade Canada, status of Canadian professional entering the United
            States under the FTA
TN   Trade NAFTA, or NAFTA Professional
USC   United States Code

Part I

Introduction

Chapter 1

Introduction

After years of negotiations, the North American Free Trade Agreement (NAFTA)[1] came into force on January 1, 1994,[2] uniting the United States, Canada, and Mexico into one of the world's largest trading agreements. In addition to facilitating trade among the three parties to the treaty, NAFTA permits citizen business persons from any of the three countries to temporarily work in either of the other two countries. The provisions in NAFTA establish preferential trading relationships between the Parties, facilitate temporary entry on a reciprocal basis, establish transparent criteria and procedures for temporary entry, ensure border security, and protect the domestic labor force and permanent employment in their respective territories. Each of the Parties has enacted laws and procedures to implement these immigration provisions.

While NAFTA is a document with consequences for federal governments and large business, it can also have a significant impact on all businesses in the United States, from large corporations, to mid-size businesses, to sole proprietorships with one or two employees. The immigration provisions in NAFTA apply to all employers in the United States; they cover a wide spectrum of types of Canadians and Mexicans who may be employed in the United States. Many mid-size and small businesses are seeking the most highly skilled business people and other professionals available to meet the demands of rapidly changing technology and information services. Now, under NAFTA, even the smallest businesses can look to citizens of Canada and Mexico as part of their human resource pool of potential employees.

The procedures for hiring an employee under NAFTA are not too complicated or expensive for most businesses to undertake. There is, however, the requirement to prepare all petitions accurately and completely, avoid fraudulent documents and claims, and file applications with the Immigration and Naturalization Service (INS) in a timely manner.

HIRING FOREIGN PROFESSIONALS

NAFTA has certain immigration provisions in Chapter 16. In reality it has "nonimmigrant" provisions, since U.S. immigration law differentiates between immigrants who are aliens, who are granted permanent residence status, and nonimmigrants, who are granted a temporary status. NAFTA only provides for the temporary entry of citizens from Canada or Mexico to enter and work in the United States.

Basic Principles

NAFTA and U.S. immigration law have defined permissible business activities, temporary entry, employers, and citizens. They have also set some numerical restrictions on entry.

Business Activities

NAFTA includes four specific business activities for which business persons who are citizens of Canada or Mexico may enter the United States: business visitors, traders and investors, intracompany transferees, and professionals. "Business person," as defined in NAFTA, means a citizen of Canada or Mexico who is engaged in the trade of goods, the provision of services, or the conduct of investment activities.

"Business visitors" are those who make a temporary visit to the United States to engage in business activities for their employer or business in their home country. The home country business activities must be international in scope, and the entry of the business visitor must not involve employment in the United States. For a complete discussion see Chapter 2.

"Traders and investors" are business persons who want to do one of the following: (1) carry on substantial trade in goods or services principally between the country where the business person is a citizen and the United States; or (2) establish, develop, administer, or provide advice or key technical services to the operation of an investment to which the business person or his or her foreign company has committed, or is in the process of committing, a substantial amount of capital. The trader or investor must be in a capacity that is supervisory, executive, or involves essential skills. See Chapter 3 for a complete discussion.

An "intracompany transferee" is a business person employed by a business in Canada or Mexico who wants to provide services to that business or to a subsidiary or affiliate in the United States, in a capacity that is managerial, executive, or involves specialized knowledge. See Chapter 4 for a complete discussion.

"Business activities at a professional level" means those occupations that require at least a baccalaureate degree or appropriate credentials demonstrating status as a professional. "Engage in business activities at a professional level" means to perform prearranged business activities for a U.S. entity, including an individual. NAFTA does not authorize the establishment of a business or practice in the United States in which a professional will be self-employed. A professional person can only enter the United States under NAFTA to work full- or part-time for an employer. See the chapters in Part III.

Temporary Entry

NAFTA provides that professionals and other business persons will enter the United States only on a temporary basis. This is shown even by the title to Chapter 16 of NAFTA, which is "Temporary Entry for Business Persons." The general principles of Chapter 16 of NAFTA are to facilitate temporary entry on a reciprocal basis, to establish transparent criteria and procedures for temporary entry, and to protect the domestic labor force and permanent employment in each territory.

"Temporary entry" means entry without the intent to establish permanent residence and for a period that has a defined end. Persons entering on a temporary basis are nonimmigrants in U.S. law and must file the required forms for entry and obtain the appropriate nonimmigrant status. When applying for any status under NAFTA at a port of entry or consular office, the applicant must satisfy the INS officer or consular officer that his or her proposed stay will be temporary. While the Foreign Affairs Manual, which sets the procedures for U.S. consular officers to follow, does not set out any procedures for determining the intent of the applicant, a consular officer must determine that the circumstances surrounding an application reasonably and convincingly indicate that the alien's temporary work assignment in the United States will end predictably, and that the alien will depart. If the alien does not convince the consular officer that he or she only wants to enter for a temporary period of time, the consular officer can and will refuse the visa and entry. There is an exception for those entering in L-1 status, however: they may have a dual intent of entering the United States for a temporary job and later or concurrently applying for permanent residence.

There is no rule that requires that an applicant under NAFTA show that he or she has a foreign residence, but it is usually suggested that applicants from Mexico should have documentation to present at a U.S. consulate showing ties to Mexico that indicate an intention to return to a home there after their temporary entry to the United States.

Employer Requirements

Business visitors will not be employed in the United States but must be employed or receive their remuneration from a source in their home country. Traders and investors are restricted to employment with the operation or investment that qualifies the trader or investor for this nonimmigrant status. Intracompany transferees are restricted to being employed by their foreign employer or by a U.S. subsidiary or affiliate of that employer.

There is a difference as to who qualifies to be a employer of a Mexican or Canadian Trade NAFTA (TN) professional. Canadian citizens may seek entry to the United States in TN status to engage in business activities for a U.S. employer or entity. Canadians may also obtain TN status if they work for a foreign employer that will provide prearranged services to a U.S. entity. There is no rule that the foreign employer be Canadian. If the foreign employer is a Canadian corporation, the Canadian citizen providing service to the U.S. entity might qualify for a L-1 visa if his or her job duties can be defined as those of a multinational executive or manager.

Mexican citizens who seek entry as a TN professional may only have a U.S. employer make a job offer.

The employer may be a corporation, a partnership, an organization, or an individual. NAFTA specifically does not authorize a Canadian or Mexican citizen professional to establish a business or practice in the United States in which the professional will be self-employed.

Citizenship

Professionals entering under NAFTA from Canada and Mexico must be citizens of their respective country. Annex 1608 of NAFTA defines a citizen of Mexico as a national or a citizen according to the existing provisions of Articles 30 and 34 of the Mexican Constitution. According to Mexican law, Mexican nationality is acquired by birth or by naturalization, while citizens are Mexicans who have the status of Mexicans and meet the requirements of having reached the age of eighteen and having an honest means of livelihood.[3] There is no definition for Canadian citizens in NAFTA, but they include those born in Canada and those who have received Canadian citizenship through naturalization.

While the applicant for TN status must be a citizen, there is no rule requiring that the spouse and children who accompany or follow the TN alien also be citizens. A non-citizen who has married a Canadian or Mexican citizen is entitled to accompany or follow the citizen spouse and obtain Trade Dependent (TD) status. See Chapter 10.

Otherwise Qualified for Entry

Each party to NAFTA is required to allow temporary entry to professionals who qualify under NAFTA who are otherwise qualified for entry under applicable measures relating to public health and safety and national security. They must also comply with existing immigration measures applicable to temporary entry. This means that every NAFTA applicant must meet all of the requirements as to health-related issues, criminal convictions, security, public charge, immigration violations, and eligibility for citizenship, and comply with all the documentation requirements. The application procedure for Canadian citizens generally does not include questions about, or an investigation into, these issues. It appears that only issues that are obvious (such as indications of poor health) or anything that is noted on the INS computer system when the Canadian arrives at a port of entry, or when the NAFTA application information is added to the computer system, will be investigated. If it is discovered that the Canadian citizen who has been issued a TN approval does not meet the qualification requirement, the director of INS may be able to revoke the approval. However, there is no specific rule allowing this.

Numerical Restrictions

During the negotiations for NAFTA there was concern from labor unions that there would be large numbers of Mexican professionals entering the United States. There are no numerical restrictions on B-1, E-1, E-2, or L-1 visas. However, NAFTA contains provisions that any country, after consultation, may establish an annual numerical limit regarding temporary entry of professionals of another Party. The United States and Mexico agreed to an annual limit of 5,500 initial petitions of business persons from Mexico seeking temporary entry to engage in a business activity at a professional level in one of the approved professions. The 5,500 numerical limit must not take into account the renewal of a period of temporary entry, the entry of a spouse or child accompanying or following to join the principal business person, admission of Mexican professionals under the Immigration and Nationality Act (INA) section for H-1B professionals,[4] or an admission under any other provision of the INA section relating to the entry of professionals.

Starting with the effective date of NAFTA, not more than 5,500 citizens of Mexico can be classified as TN nonimmigrants annually. Each Mexican citizen who obtains a TN visa is counted for the numerical limit, but applicants for TN extensions and the spouse or children of a Mexican TN are not counted. A temporary number is assigned to each application for TN classification for a Mexican citizen, and if the petition is denied, the number is returned to the system to be assigned to a new petition. Likewise, numbers are returned to the system to be reassigned to new petitions if the recipient of an approved petition does not apply for admission to the United States and notifies the service center director who approved the petition. If the total annual limit is reached prior to the end of the year, new petitions and the accompanying fee will be rejected and returned to

Figure 1.1
Number of Canadian and Mexican Nonimmigrants Entering the United States
under NAFTA[1]

Category	Total	Canada	Mexico
1994			
All categories	391,181	70,216	320,965
B-1	340,676	24,455	316,221
E-1	309	187	122
E-2	3,114	2,877	237
L-1	9,425	6,617	2,808
L-2	5,819	4,269	1,550
TN	25,120	25,104	16
TD	6,718	6,707	11
1995			
All categories	326,594	70,500	256,094
B-1	272,818	22, 988	249,830
E-1	350	185	165
E-2	3,001	2,481	520
L-1	10,918	7,386	3,532
L-2	6,397	4,426	1,971
TN	25,661	25,598	63
TD	7,449	7,436	13

[1]Information received in a telephone conversation with Helen deThomas, Adjudications Officer, Business and Trade Services Branch, Benefits Division, INS Headquarters, October
17, 1996.

the applicant with a notice that numbers are unavailable for Mexican citizen TN applicants. The date when numbers will again be available will
also be supplied. The INS fiscal year is from October 1 to September 30.

The annual numerical limit for Mexican citizen TN nonimmigrants can
be increased or decreased by agreement between the United States and
Mexico and will expire ten years after the date of entry into force of
NAFTA. The concern about a flood of Mexican professionals entering as
TN nonimmigrants has not proved to be true. During the first two years
of entry of TN nonimmigrants under NAFTA, the number of Mexican
citizens among them has been extremely small. In 1994 there were 25,120
TN nonimmigrants—25,104 from Canada and only 16 from Mexico. In
1995 there was a total of 25,661 TN nonimmigrants—25,598 from Canada and only 63 from Mexico (see Figure 1.1). It is unknown why the num-

ber of Mexican TN nonimmigrants is so low; it is possible that the more complicated application procedure for Mexican citizens has discouraged applications.

NOTES

1. North American Free Trade Agreement between the Government of the United States of America, the Government of Canada, and the Government of the United Mexican States, 1993, herein referred to as NAFTA.

2. North American Free Trade Implementation Act, Pub.L. No. 103-182, 107 Stat. 2057.

3. NAFTA, Article 34, at page 36.

4. INA § 101(a)(15)(H)(i)(b) and § 214(g)(1)(A), which establish worldwide limits.

Part II

Business Persons under NAFTA

Chapter 2

Business Visitors

Business visitors are defined in NAFTA as citizens of a Party who are engaged in trade in goods, the provision of services, or the conduct of investment activities. Business visitors are not allowed to work in the United States, and therefore cannot be hired or employed by U.S. employers. This category is included in this book for completeness, and because employers may have dealings with business visitors at trade shows, during research programs, as sales or distribution people, or as providers of after-sales service. It can be useful to a U.S. business executive to understand the types of work business visitors can perform and how long they can stay in the United States.

DEFINITION OF BUSINESS VISITOR

A business visitor, as defined in NAFTA, is a citizen of a Party who is engaged in trade in goods, the provision of services, or the conduct of investment activities. The INA creates a category for B^1 visa visitors and defines them as aliens who have a residence in a foreign country that they have no intention of abandoning and who are visiting the United States temporarily for business.

Citizens of Canada or Mexico who want to enter the United States for business, and who are otherwise eligible to obtain a B-1 visa, may be classified as nonimmigrant B-1 visitors if they meet the criteria set out in the INA or in NAFTA. Engaging in business for a B-1 visa classification generally means the person will be engaged in business activities other than the performance of skilled or unskilled labor. Therefore, the issuance of a B-1 visa is not intended for the purpose of obtaining and engaging in employment while in the United States and does not permit the B-1 visitor to accept employment.

NAFTA, in Appendix 1603.A.1, sets out seven areas of business that a business visitor may undertake. These include:

1. *Research and Design*

Technical, scientific, and statistical researchers conducting independent research or research for an enterprise located in the territory of another Party.

2. *Growth, Manufacture, and Production*

Harvester owner supervising a harvesting crew admitted under applicable law. This applies only to harvesting of agricultural crops of grain, fiber, fruit, and vegetables.

Purchasing and production management personnel conducting commercial transactions for an enterprise located in the territory of another Party.

3. *Marketing*

Market researchers and analysts conducting independent research or analysis, or research or analysis for an enterprise located in the territory of another Party.

Trade fair and promotional personnel attending a trade convention.

4. *Sales*

Sales representatives and agents taking orders or negotiating contracts for goods or services for an enterprise located in the territory of another Party but not delivering goods or providing services.

Buyers purchasing for an enterprise located in the territory of another Party.

5. *Distribution*

Transportation operators transporting goods or passengers to the territory of a Party from the territory of another Party, or loading and transporting goods or passengers from the territory of a Party, with no unloading in that territory, to the territory of another Party. These operators may make deliveries in the United States if all goods or passengers to be delivered were loaded in the territory of another Party. Furthermore, they may load from locations in U.S. if all goods or passengers to be loaded will be delivered in the territory of another Party. Purely domestic service or solicitation, in competition with U.S. operators, is not permitted.

With respect to temporary entry into the territory of the United States, Canadian customs brokers performing brokerage duties relating to the export of goods from the territory of the United States, to, or through, the territory of Canada.

With respect to temporary entry into the territory of Canada, U.S. customs brokers performing brokerage duties relating to the export of goods from the territory of Canada to, or through, the territory of the United States.

Customs brokers providing consulting services regarding the facilitation of the import or export of goods.

6. *After-Sales Service*

Installers, repair and maintenance personnel, and supervisors, possessing specialized knowledge essential to a seller's contractual obligation, who are performing services or training workers to perform services, pursuant to a warranty or other service contract incidental to the sale of commercial or industrial equipment or machinery, including computer software, purchased from an enterprise located outside the territory of the Party into which temporary entry is sought, during the life of the warranty or service agreement. For the purposes of this provision, the commercial or industrial equipment or machinery, including computer software, must have been manufactured outside the United States.

7. *General Service*

Professionals engaging in a business activity at a professional level in a profession set out in Appendix 1603.D.1 who receive no salary or other remuneration from a U.S. source other than an expense allowance or other reimbursement for expenses incidental to the temporary stay.

Management and supervisory personnel engaging in a commercial transaction for an enterprise located in the territory of another Party.

Financial services personnel (insurers, bankers, or investment brokers) engaging in commercial transactions for an enterprise located in the territory of another Party.

Public relations and advertising personnel consulting with business associates, or attending or participating in conventions.

Tourism personnel (tour and travel agents, tour guides, or tour operators) attending or participating in conventions or conducting a tour that has begun in the territory of another Party. The tour may begin in the United States, but must terminate in foreign territory, and a significant portion of the tour must be conducted in foreign territory. In such a case, an operator may enter the United States with an empty conveyance, and a tour guide may enter on his or her own and join the conveyance.

Tour bus operators entering the territory of a Party (a) with a group of passengers on a bus tour that has begun in, and will return to, the territory of another Party; (b) to meet a group of passengers on a bus tour that will end, and the predominant portion of which will take place, in the territory of another Party; or (c) with a group of passengers on a bus tour to be unloaded in the territory of the Party into which temporary entry is sought, and returning with no passengers or reloading with the group for transportation to the territory of another Party.

Translators or interpreters performing services as employees of an enterprise located in the territory of another Party.

These are not the only occupations and professions that may enter as a business visitor under NAFTA, however. Nothing precludes a business person who engages in any other business or occupation from temporary entry with a B-1 status if he or she meets all the other requirements for admission. There is one exception. Construction workers are specifically excluded from such temporary entry, but supervisors or trainers of workers engaged in building or construction work are eligible for B-1 status as long as they don't actually perform building or construction work themselves.

Other business activities that are permitted for the issuance of a B-1 visa include the following:

1. *Participants in Voluntary Service Programs.* Aliens who participate in a voluntary service program that benefits U.S. local communities may receive a B-1 visa. They must show that they are members of, and have a commitment to, a particular recognized religious or nonprofit charitable organization and that they will not receive a salary or any other type of remuneration from a U.S. source. They may receive an allowance or other reimbursement for expenses incidental to their stay in the United States. A voluntary service program is an organized project conducted by a recognized religious or nonprofit charitable organization to provide assistance to the poor or the needy or to further a religious or charitable cause. The program may not, however, sell articles or solicit or accept donations. The recognized religious or nonprofit charitable organization must prove that the voluntary program meets the INS definition of voluntary service program. It must also show that it meets other criteria set out in the INA with regard to voluntary workers. The applicant must provide a written statement issued by the sponsoring organization for attachment to the visa for presentation to the INS officer at the port of entry. The written statement must contain INS required information such as

a. The volunteer's name, and date and place of birth;

b. The foreign permanent residence address;

c. The name and address of initial destination in the United States; and

d. The anticipated duration of assignment.

2. *Members of Board of Directors of U.S. Corporation.* An alien who is a member of the board of directors of a U.S. corporation who wants to enter the United States to attend a meeting of the board or to perform other functions resulting from membership on the board qualifies for a B-1 visa.

3. *Servants of Foreign Nationals in Nonimmigrant Status.* Personal or domestic servants who accompany or follow to join their employer who is applying for admission into, or who is already in, the United States in certain nonimmigrant status may obtain a B-1 visa to continue to work for their employer, if

a. The employee has a residence abroad that he or she has no intention of abandoning (notwithstanding the fact that the employer may be in a nonimmigrant status that does not require such a showing);

b. The employee can demonstrate at least one year's experience as a personal or domestic servant;

c. The employee has been employed abroad by the employer as a personal or domestic servant, for at least one year prior to the date of the employer's admission to the United States, or if the employee-employer relationship existed immediately prior to the time of visa application, the employer can demonstrate that he or she has regularly employed (either year-round or seasonally) personal or domestic servants over a period of several years preceding the domestic servant's visa application for a nonimmigrant B-1 visa; and

d. The employer and the employee have signed an employment contract that contains statements that the employer guarantees the employee the minimum or prevailing wages, whichever is greater, and free room and board, and will be the only provider of employment to the servant.

4. *Professional Athletes.* Athletes who may obtain a B-1 visa include

a. Professional athletes, such as golfers and auto racers, who receive no salary or payment other than prize money for their participation in a tournament or sporting event.

b. Athletes or team members who want to enter the United States as members of a foreign-based team to compete with another sports team. To qualify, the foreign athlete and the foreign sports team must have their principal place of business or activity in a foreign country; the income of the foreign-based team and the salary of its players must be principally accrued in a foreign country; and the foreign-based sports team must be a member of an international sports league or the sporting activities involved must have an international dimension.

c. Amateur hockey players who are asked to join a professional team during the course of the regular professional season or playoffs for brief tryouts. To qualify, the player must be a draft choice who has not signed professional contracts but has signed a memorandum of agreement with a National Hockey League (NHL) parent team. Under the terms of the agreement, the team must provide only for incidental expenses, such as round-trip fare, hotel room, meals, and transportation. At the time of the visa application or application for admission to the United States, the player must provide a copy of the memorandum of agreement and a letter from the NHL team giving the details of the tryouts, or if an agreement is not available at that time, a letter from the NHL team stating that such an agreement has been signed and giving the details of the tryout.

5. *Horse Race Employees.* If an owner of racing horses enters races in the United States, he or she may obtain a B-1 visa for a jockey, sulkey driver, trainer, or groom. The employer and employee must be the same nationality. The employee is not allowed to work for any other foreign or U.S. employer.

6. *Commercial or Industrial Workers.* An alien coming to the United States to install, service, or repair commercial or industrial equipment or machinery purchased from a company outside the United States, or to train U.S. workers to perform such services, is eligible for a B-1 visa. However, in such cases the contract of sale must specifically require the foreign seller to provide such services or training, and the visa applicant must possess specialized knowledge essential to the seller's contractual obligation to per-

form the services or training. The alien cannot receive any remuneration from a U.S. source. These provisions do not apply to an alien seeking to perform building or construction work, whether on-site or in-plant, except for an alien who is applying for a B-1 visa for the purpose of supervising or training other workers engaged in building or construction work, but not actually performing any such building or construction work.

7. *Foreign Airline Employees.* Aliens who seek to enter the United States for employment in an executive, supervisory, or highly technical capacity with a foreign airline engaged in international transportation of passengers and freight, who cannot obtain an E visa because there is no treaty of friendship, commerce, and navigation in effect between the United States and the country of the aliens' nationality or because they are not nationals of the airline's country of nationality may obtain a B-1 visa. Employees of foreign airlines coming to the United States to pick up aircraft may also be documented as B-1 visitors, since they are not transiting the United States and are not admissible as crewmen. Such applicants, however, must present a letter from the foreign airline headquarters branch verifying the employment and official capacity of the applicants in the United States.

8. *Clerkships.* Except as in the cases described below, aliens who wish to obtain hands-on clerkship experience are not deemed to fall within B-1 visa classification. An alien may qualify for a Medical Clerkship provided that the alien is studying at a foreign medical school and seeks to enter the United States temporarily in order to take an "elective clerkship" at a U.S. medical school's hospital without remuneration from the hospital. An "elective clerkship" provides practical experience and instruction in the various disciplines of medicine under the supervision and direction of faculty physicians at a U.S. medical school's hospital as an approved part of the alien's foreign medical school education.

9. *Aliens Observing Business or Other Professional or Vocational Activities.* An alien who is coming to the United States merely and exclusively to observe the conduct of business or other professional or vocational activity may be classified B-1, provided the alien pays for his or her own expenses. However, aliens, often students, who seek to gain practical experience must qualify under other sections of the INA.

10. *Aliens Employed by Foreign or U.S. Exhibitors at International Fairs or Expositions.* Aliens who are coming to the United States to plan, construct, dismantle, maintain, or be employed in connection with exhibits at international fairs or expositions may, depending upon the circumstances in each case, qualify for a B-1 visa.

11. *Still Photographers.* The Immigration and Naturalization Service permits still photographers to enter the United States with B-1 visas for the purpose of taking photographs as long as they receive no income from a U.S. source.

12. *Musicians.* An alien musician may be issued a B-1 visa, provided the musician is coming to the United States to utilize recording facilities for recording purposes only, the recording will be distributed and sold only outside the United States, and no public performances will be given.

13. *Medical Doctors.* A medical doctor whose purpose for coming to the United States is to observe U.S. medical practices and consult with colleagues on the latest techniques, provided no remuneration is received from a U.S. source and no patient care is involved can enter on a B-1 visa. Failure to pass the Foreign Medical Graduate Examination (FMGE) is irrelevant in such a case.

14. *Artists.* An artist coming to the United States to paint, sculpt, or engage in similar artistic activities who is not under contract with a U.S. employer and who does not intend to regularly sell such artwork in the United States, can enter the United States with a B-1 visa.

15. *Members of Religious Organizations.* Ministers of religion proceeding to the United States to engage in an evangelical tour who do not plan to take an appointment with any one church, and who will be supported by offerings contributed at each evangelical meeting, may obtain a B-1 visa.

16. *Ministers of Religion Exchanging Pulpits.* Ministers of religion temporarily exchanging pulpits with American counterparts who will continue to be reimbursed by the foreign church and will draw no salary from the host church in the United States also qualify for a B-1 visa.

17. *Missionary Workers.* Members of religious denominations, whether ordained or not, who enter the United States temporarily for the sole purpose of performing missionary work on behalf of a denomination may qualify for a B-1 visa. The work must not involve the selling of articles or the solicitation or acceptance of donations. The minister must not receive a salary or remuneration from a U.S. source other than an expense allowance or other reimbursement for expenses incidental to the temporary stay. Missionary work for this purpose may include religious instruction, aid to the elderly or needy, proselytizing, and similar activities. It does not include ordinary administrative work, nor can it be used as a substitute for ordinary labor for hire.

ADMISSION PROCEDURE AND REQUIREMENTS

Citizens of Canada and Mexico who seek temporary admission with a B-1 visa cannot be required to obtain employment authorization as long as they comply with the provisions for entry under this status. No prior approval procedure, labor certification tests, or other procedures are, or may be, required. There are no numerical restrictions on the number of business visitors entering the United States.

Evidence Required

An applicant for a B-1 visa who is a Canadian citizen must present proof of citizenship, and a Mexican citizen must present a valid entry document, such as a passport and visa or a Mexican Border Crossing Card. Both must present documentation that they will be engaged in a business activity, describe the purpose of their entry, and present evidence that the proposed business activity is international in scope and that they are not seeking to enter the local labor market. To show this, the applicant may demonstrate that his or her primary source of remuneration for the proposed business activity is outside the United States and that his or her principal place of business and actual place of accrual of profits, at least predominantly, remain outside the United States. Usually an oral declaration about the location of the principal place of business and actual place of accrual of profits will be sufficient. If the examining officer desires further evidence, usually a letter from the employer will be sufficient.

PERIOD OF STAY

Generally, business visitors, like visitors for pleasure (tourists), may be admitted to the United States for up to one year. However, the minimum period of admission is for six months, and anyone who is eligible for a B-1 visa will be issued a visa for that period of time, regardless of whether that time is requested or not. B-1 visa holders can be granted extensions of their temporary stay in increments of up to six months.

To obtain an extension of stay, the business visitor may apply from within the United States by filing INS form I-539 at the Service Center having jurisdiction where the business visitor lives in the United States. The completed form I-539 must be filed with

1. The appropriate fee.
2. Details of the reason for the extension, including why the stay will be temporary and the details of the arrangements made to depart the United States.
3. Details on any effect of the extended stay on the business visitor's foreign employment and residency.
4. A copy of both sides of the business visitor's I-94.

Generally, Canadian citizens are not issued an I-94 when entering at a northern port of entry. This will likely change in the future as provisions regarding departure documents of the 1996 act are enacted.

The petition to extend the stay should be filed at least 45 days before the current stay expires to give the Service Center adequate time to evaluate the petition and respond. If a petition to extend the stay is not filed early, the business visitor may become out of status before receiving an extension. Failure to file before the expiration date may be excused if the petitioner demonstrates when filing the petition that the delay was due to extraordinary circumstances beyond his or her control, that the length of delay was reasonable, that the applicant did not otherwise violate his or her status, that the applicant is still a bona fide nonimmigrant, and that the applicant is not in deportation proceedings.

SPOUSE AND CHILDREN

The spouse and children of a business visitor may enter, if they meet all other qualifications, as a B-2 visitor for pleasure.

NOTE

1. There are two categories of B visas. B-1 is for a business visitor. B-2 is for a visitor for pleasure, a tourist.

Chapter 3

Treaty Traders and Treaty Investors

A visa classification has been provided specifically for people involved in International Trade and Investment. These visas are known as treaty trader and treaty investor visas, or E-1 and E-2 respectively. Treaty traders are defined in NAFTA as citizens of a Party who are business persons seeking to carry on substantial trade in goods or services principally between the territory of the Party of which they are a citizen and the territory of the Party into which entry is sought.[1] Treaty investors are defined in NAFTA as citizens of a Party who are business persons seeking to establish, develop, administer, or provide advice or key technical services to the operation of an investment to which they or their enterprise has committed, or is in the process of committing, a substantial amount of capital in a company.[2]

Treaty traders and treaty investors are allowed to work in the United States only for a qualifying entity; they can not be hired or employed by U.S. employers. This category is included in this book for completeness, and because employers may themselves be a "qualifying entity" or may have dealings with some treaty traders or treaty investors at trade shows, during research programs, or as sales or distribution people. It can be useful to a U.S. business executive of a qualifying entity to understand the types of work treaty trader or treaty investor visitors can perform and how long they can stay in the United States. It should be noted that a treaty visa is not a substitute for immigrant status, even though the person may remain in the United States almost indefinitely.

TREATY TRADER E-1

The treaty trader visa is designed for entities or individuals who develop substantial trade between the United States and a country with which the

United States maintains a treaty. NAFTA is such a treaty that makes treaty trader status available to Canadian and Mexican citizens. The INA creates a category for E-1 visa holders[3] and defines them as having a residence in a foreign country that they have no intention of abandoning and as visiting the United States temporarily for business. NAFTA, in Appendix 1603, section B, further states that this status under the treaty is applicable only to temporary entry. Though only allowed for a temporary entry, the E-1 visa does not require the holder to establish intent to proceed to the United States for a specific temporary period of time. Nor does the E-1 visa holder need to have a residence in a foreign country that the beneficiary does not tend to abandon. The foreign visa holder's expression of an unequivocal intent to return when the E status ends is normally sufficient, in the absence of specific indications of evidence that the visa holder's intent is to the contrary.

Since NAFTA is a treaty of trade, the U.S. office of the company must engage in substantial international trade. A substantial proportion (at least 51 percent) of the trade must be between the United States and Canada, or the United States and Mexico. Trade involves the actual exchange of goods, monies, or services and is generally demonstrated to exist by the number of transactions as well as by dollar volume.

Treaty trader visas are available to managers, executives, or individuals with specific skills that are not generally available in the U.S. work force and that make their presence essential to the efficient operation of the enterprise. Unskilled manual workers, clerical workers, or middle and lower management personnel do not qualify.

Trade in goods includes both exports and imports between the United States and Canada or the United States and Mexico. Trade in monies and services has been interpreted to include international banking, insurance, transportation, tourism, communications, data processing, advertising, accounting, design and engineering, management consulting, and newsgathering activities. Applicants engaged in newsgathering activities, however, should usually receive I visa classification.

Complying with the specific requirements of the treaty and the INS regulations requires a detailed understanding of the qualifications for treaty trader status and the activities treaty traders are allowed to engage in.

Trade

Trade for E-1 purposes consists of three ingredients, which must all be present in all E-1 cases. The three requirements are

1. Trade must constitute an exchange;
2. Trade must be international in scope; and
3. Trade must involve qualifying activities.

There must be an actual exchange of qualifying commodities, and title to the trade item must pass between the United States and either Canada or Mexico. The exchange of a good or service for consideration must flow between the United States and either Canada or Mexico. Qualifying activities include the exchange of goods, moneys, or services to constitute transactions considered trade within the meaning of the act.[4]

Trade Must Be International

One of the purposes of NAFTA is to develop international commercial trade between the parties. Development of the domestic market without international exchange does not constitute trade in the E-1 visa context. Thus, engaging in purely domestic trade is not contemplated under this classification. The traceable exchange in goods or services must be between the United States and either Canada or Mexico.

Trade Must Be in Existence

An alien cannot qualify for E-1 status for the purpose of searching for a trading relationship. Trade between Mexico or Canada and the United States must already be in progress on behalf of the individual or firm to entitle the individual or firm to treaty trader classification. Existing trade includes successfully integrated contracts binding upon the parties that call for the immediate exchange of qualifying items of trade.

Activities Considered to Constitute Trade

Trade for E-1 visa purposes involves the commercial exchange of goods or services in the international market place. In today's rapidly changing business climate with its increasing trend toward service industries, many more services, whether listed in this chapter or not, might benefit from E-1 visa classification. To constitute trade in a service for E-1 purposes, the provision of that service by an enterprise must be the purpose of that business and, most importantly, must itself be the saleable commodity that the enterprise sells to clients. The term trade as used in the INA has been interpreted to include international banking, insurance, transportation, tourism, communications, and newsgathering activities. (Aliens engaged in newsgathering activities, however, should usually be classified under an I visa). These activities do not constitute an all-inclusive list but are merely examples of the types of services found to fall within the E-1 meaning of trade.

Substantial Trade

The word "substantial" is intended to describe the flow of the goods or services that are being exchanged between the treaty countries. That is, the trade must be a continuous flow and should involve numerous transactions over time. An applicant for an E-1 visa should focus primarily on the volume of trade conducted, in addition to the monetary value of the transactions. Although the number of transactions and the value of each transaction will vary, greater weight is accorded to cases involving more numerous transactions of larger value. The smaller business person will not be excluded if he or she can demonstrate a pattern of transactions of value. Thus, proof of numerous transactions, although each may be relatively small in value, might establish the requisite continuing course of international trade that is sufficient to support the treaty trader and family. This proof should be considered as a favorable factor when assessing the substantiality of trade in a particular case.

Trade Must Be Principally between United States and Country of Alien's Nationality

The general rule requires that at least 51 percent of the total volume of the international trade conducted by the treaty trader, regardless of location, must be between the United States and either Canada or Mexico, whichever is the treaty country of the alien's nationality. The remainder of the trade in which the alien is engaged may be international trade with other countries or domestic trade. A number of factors are considered in making a determination of the value of trade.

Measurement of Trade

To measure the requisite trade, it is essential to look at the trade conducted by the legal person that is the treaty trader. Such a trader might be an individual, which was often the case many years ago, a partnership, a joint venture, or a corporation (either a parent or subsidiary corporation). It is important to note that a branch of a company is not considered to be a separate legal person or trader but part and parcel of another entity. In contrast, a subsidiary is a separate legal person or entity. Therefore, to measure trade in the case of a branch, the person seeking E-1 status must focus on the trade conducted by the entity of which the branch is a part, which is usually a foreign-based business (individual or corporation). A branch may have substantial international trade, but because of its legal structure, the amount of trade to be measured is the total trade of the company and not just the branch. As a result of looking at all of the trade, the amount may not be substantial with respect to qualifying for an E-1 visa.

Effect on Employee's Responsibilities in the United States

If the trader, whether foreign-based or U.S.-based, meets this percentage requirement, the duties of an employee need not be similarly apportioned to qualify for an E-1 visa. For example, if a U.S. subsidiary of a foreign firm is engaged principally in trade between the United States and the treaty country, it is not material that the E-1 employee is also engaged in third-country or intra-U.S. trade or that the parent firm's headquarters abroad is engaged primarily in trade with other countries. This would not be true in the case of a branch of a foreign firm.

TREATY INVESTOR E-2

Treaty investors are defined in NAFTA as citizens of a Party who are business persons seeking to establish, develop, administer, or provide advice or key technical services to, the operation of an investment to which the business person or the business person's enterprise has committed, or is in the process of committing, a substantial amount of capital in a company.

The treaty investor visa is designed for entities or individuals who invest, or are in the active process of investing, substantial funds in the United States. These investments need not be in the area of international trade. The treaty investor visa is only available to individuals who are nationals of countries with which the United States maintains a treaty of commerce and navigation. NAFTA is such a treaty, thus making available the E-2 visa to Canadian and Mexican citizens. Since this is a treaty designed in part to further bilateral investment, the Canadian or Mexican investing entity or individual must have substantial funds available for investment. A substantial investment is generally defined as more than half the value of the U.S. enterprise or more than half the amount necessary to establish a new enterprise of the type contemplated. In addition, the investment must not be marginal. The concept of marginality means an investment that will generate little more than a living income for the investor. The entity or individual requesting treaty investor registration must be in a position to develop and direct the enterprise in the United States, which requires control of more than 50 percent of the U.S. enterprise.

Applicants for treaty investor status will be required to document the monies and goods invested in the United States, the ownership and anticipated revenues of the investment, and the total number of employees.

Individual investors and executive or managerial personnel may be found eligible for the treaty investor visa. Other employees qualify only if they possess specialist skills that are not readily available on the U.S. labor market and are essential to the U.S. operations of the investment enterprise. In addition, technical personnel may qualify if they are required for the establishment of the enterprise; for the training or supervision of technicians employed in manufacturing, maintenance, or repair functions; or for the continuous development of product improvements and quality control. Low-level managers and employees who perform routine substantive job duties, such as unskilled manual workers or clerical workers, do not qualify.

Complying with the specific requirements of the treaty and the INS regulations involves a number of elements.

The Concept of Investment and in Process of Investing

The nature of the investment transaction is critical to the determination of whether a particular financial arrangement may be considered an investment within the meaning of the treaty. The core factors relevant to whether the petitioner has actually invested, or is in the process of investing, in an enterprise are discussed below.

Possession and Control of Funds

The alien must demonstrate possession and control of the funds invested. If the investor has received the funds by legitimate means, for example, savings, gift, inheritance, or contest winnings, and has control and possession over the funds, the proper employment of the funds may constitute an E-2 investment. It should be noted, however, that inheritance of a business in the United States does not constitute an investment. Furthermore, the statute does not require that the source of the funds be outside the United States.

Investment Connotes Risk

The concept of investment connotes the placing of funds or other capital assets at risk, in the commercial sense, in the hope of generating a financial return. Because of this requirement, E-2 investor status cannot be extended to non-profit organizations. If the funds are not subject to partial or total loss if business fortunes reverse, then it is not an investment in the sense intended by the U.S. law.

If the availability of funds arises from indebtedness, the investor must still be at risk for the investment. Indebtedness such as mortgage debt or commercial loans secured by the assets of the enterprise cannot count toward the investment, as there is no requisite element of risk. For example, if the business in which the alien is investing is used as collateral, funds from the resulting loan or mortgage are not at risk, even if some personal assets are also used as collateral. On the other hand, loans secured by the alien's own personal assets (such as a second mortgage on a home) or unsecured loans (such as a loan on the alien's personal signature) may be included, since the alien risks the funds in the event of business failure. In short, at-risk funds in the E-2 context would include only funds in which personal assets are involved, such as personal funds, other unencumbered assets, or a mortgage with the alien's personal liability. A reasonable amount of cash, held in a business bank account or similar fund to be used for routine business operations, may be counted as investment funds.

Funds Must Be Irrevocably Committed

To be in the process of investing for E-2 purposes, the investors must have funds or assets committed to the investment, and the commitment must be real and irrevocable. For example, a purchase of a business that qualifies for E-2 status in every respect may be conditioned upon the issuance of the visa. Despite the condition, this would constitute a solid commitment if the assets to be used for the purchase were held in escrow, for release or transfer only on the condition being met. The point of the example is that to be in the process of investing the investor must have, and in this case would have, reached an irrevocable point to qualify. Moreover, for the alien to be in the process of investing, the alien must be close to the start of actual business operations, not simply in the stage of signing contracts (which may be broken) or scouting for suitable locations and property. Mere intent to invest, or possession of uncommitted funds in a bank account, or even prospective investment arrangements entailing no present commitment, will not suffice.

Consideration of Other Financial Transactions as Investments

Payments in the form of leases or rents for property or equipment may be calculated toward the investment in an amount limited to the funds devoted to that item in any one month. However, the market value of the leased equipment is not representative of the investment, and neither is the annual rental cost (unless it has been paid in advance), as these rents are generally paid from the current earnings of the business.

Value of Goods or Equipment as Investment

The amount spent for purchase of equipment and for inventory on hand may be calculated in the investment total. The value of goods or equipment transferred to the United States (such as factory machinery shipped to the United States to start or enlarge a plant) is considered an investment, provided the alien can demonstrate that the goods or machinery will be put, or are being put, to use in an ongoing commercial enterprise. The applicant must establish that the purchased goods or equipment are for business, not personal, purposes.

Commercial Enterprise Must Be Real and Active

The enterprise must be a real and active commercial or entrepreneurial undertaking, producing some service or commodity. It cannot be a paper organization or an idle speculative investment held for potential appreciation in value, such as underdeveloped land or stocks held by an investor without the intent to direct the enterprise. The investment must be a commercial enterprise; thus it must be for profit, eliminating non-profit organizations from consideration.

Investment Must Be Substantial

There is no set dollar figure that constitutes a minimum amount of investment to be considered substantial for E-2 visa purposes. This requirement is met by satisfying the proportionality test. This test is a comparison between two figures: the amount of qualifying funds invested and the cost of an established business or, if a newly created business, the cost of establishing such a business. The factors that are considered include:

1. The amount of the funds or assets actually invested must be from qualifying funds and assets as explained above.
2. The cost of an established business is generally its purchase price, which is normally considered to be the fair market value.
3. The cost of a newly created business is the actual cost needed to establish such a business to the point of being operational. The actual cost can usually be computed, as the investor should have already purchased at least some of the necessary assets and thus be able to provide cost figures for additional assets needed to run the business. For example, an indication of the nature and extent of commitment to a business venture may be provided by invoices or contracts for substantial purchases of equipment and inventory; appraisals of the market value of land, buildings, equipment, and machinery; accounting audits; and records required by various governmental authorities. The petitioner may need to provide additional evidence to help establish what would be a reasonable amount. Such evidence may include letters from chambers of commerce or statistics from trade associations. Unverified and unaudited financial statements based exclusively on information supplied by an applicant normally are insufficient to establish the nature and status of an enterprise.

Value of Business Determined by Nature of Business

The value (cost) of the business is clearly dependent on the nature of the enterprise. Any manufacturing business, such as an automobile manufacturer, might easily cost many millions of dollars to either purchase, or establish and operate. At the extreme opposite pole, the cost to purchase an ongoing commercial enterprise or to establish a service business, such as a consulting firm, may be relatively low. As long as all the other requirements for E-2 status are met, the cost of the business per se is not independently relevant or determinative of qualification for E-2 status.

Proportionality Test

The amount invested in the enterprise should be compared to the cost (value) of the business by comparing the amount of the investment to the cost of the business. If the two figures are the same, then the investor has invested 100 percent of the needed funds in the business. Such an investment is substantial. The vast majority of cases involve lesser percentages. The proportionality test can best be understood as a sort of inverted sliding scale. The lower the cost of the business the higher a percentage of investment is required, whereas a highly expensive business would require a lower percentage of qualifying investment. The following examples are provided only to demonstrate the concept of the test and are not to be viewed as bright-line requirements. Assessing proportionality requires the use of judgment that takes into account the totality of the factors involved; it is not a simple arithmetic exercise.

1. A newly-created business, for example, a consulting firm, might only need a $50,000 investment to be set up and to become fully operational. As this cost figure is relatively low, a higher percentage of investment is anticipated. An investment approaching 90 to 100 percent would easily meet the test.

2. A business costing $100,000 might require an investment of 75 to 100 percent to meet the test.

3. A small business costing $500,000 would generally demand upwards of a 60 percent investment, with a $375,000 investment clearly meeting the test.

4. In the case of a million dollar business, a lesser percentage might be needed, but a 50 to 60 percent investment would qualify.

5. A business requiring $10 million to purchase or establish would require a much lower percentage. A $3 million investment might suffice in view of the sheer magnitude of the dollar amount invested.

6. An investment of $10 million in a $100 million business would qualify based on the sheer magnitude of the investment itself.

Enterprise Must Be More than Marginal

Where the alien is the petitioner, as compared to a company or employer petitioning for an alien, the petitioner must not be investing in a marginal enterprise solely for the purpose of earning a living. An alien petitioner is not entitled to E-2 classification if the investment, even if substantial, will return only enough income to provide a living for the alien and his or her family. There are various ways to determine whether an investment is marginal, in the sense of only providing a livelihood for the alien.

1. First, the alien's income or financial situation must be reviewed. If the alien has another source of income or other financial means to support him or herself and the family, then the business is not deemed to be established for the sole purpose of earning a living. Furthermore, if the income derived from the business exceeds what is necessary to support the alien and his or her family, then this too meets the test.

2. If the first test is not met, and it becomes necessary to consider other factors, the alien can look to the economic impact of the business in satisfying the test of marginality. An alien may show, for instance, that the investment will expand job opportunities locally or that the income or return from such a business will have a positive significant impact on the local economy. Such a business would likewise not be considered to be marginal.

3. The alien should remember that businesses in the start-up years or during a period following the change of ownership or management often do not generate much profit. In such cases, additional evidence will need to be presented to pass the test of marginality.

Requirements for Investor to Develop and Direct and Have Controlling Interest

An investor, in accordance with NAFTA, must be coming to develop and direct the operation of an enterprise in which the applicant is investing or has invested. To meet the develop and direct requirement, the applicant should have controlling interest in the enterprise. Controlling interest can be obtained by means of ownership or by possessing controlling management responsibilities. An equal share of the investment, such as an equal partnership, may or may not give controlling interest. In cases of foreign corporate investment in U.S.-based corporations, the focus should be less on an arithmetic formula and more on corporate practice, since control of half or less of the stock sometimes gives effective control. A joint venture may also meet the develop and direct requirement, provided that a foreign corporation can demonstrate that it has, in effect, operational control.

Control by Ownership

Ownership of at least 50 percent of the business will meet the control requirement if the owner retains full rights of control of that portion of the business and has not assigned them to another. An equal share of the investment in a joint venture or an equal partnership of two parties generally does give controlling interest if the joint venture and partner each retain full management rights and responsibilities. This arrangement is often called negative control. With each of the two parties possessing equal responsibilities, they each have the capacity of making decisions that are binding on the other party. The law has determined that an equal partnership with more than two partners would not give any of the parties control based on ownership, as the element of control would be too remote even under the negative control theory.

Control by Management

As discussed, a joint venture, or an equal partnership involving two parties, could constitute control for E-2 purposes. Modern business practices constantly introduce new business structures, however. Thus, it is difficult to list all the qualifying structures. If an investor (individual or business) has control of the business through managerial control, the requirement is met. The applicant will have to satisfy the consular officer that the investor is in the position of developing and directing the business.

The Walsh and Pollard Case

This precedent decision by the Board of Immigration Appeals[5] warrants separate discussion not just because it emphasizes established rules, but also because it has led to some confusion and misinterpretation. The thrust of the fact pattern involved the contractual arrangement between a foreign entity and a U.S. business to provide services. The facts were:

1. The foreign company promised to provide certain engineering design services which the U.S. business did not have the capacity to perform.

2. The design services were specific project-oriented services.

3. The employees of the foreign company furnished under the contract were demonstrably highly qualified to provide the needed service.

4. Pursuant to the contract, the foreign business created a subsidiary in the United States to ensure fulfillment of the contract and to service its employees. This subsidiary constituted its E-2 investment.

5. The employees who came to the U.S. entity to perform these services on-site came to fulfill certain responsibilities pursuant to that very specific design project. They did not come to the United States to fill employee vacancies of the U.S. business. It is, therefore, irrelevant that the design activities could have been performed either at the facility of the foreign entity overseas or in the United States.

This decision followed the legal guidelines on E-2 visa classification. The prominent elements are

1. When applying the substantiality test, one must focus on the nature of the business. Thus, as in this case, sometimes an investment of only a small amount of money might meet the requirement.

2. The test of develop and direct applies only to the investor(s), not to the individual employees. The individual employees may qualify as essential employees and qualify for an E-2 visa, while the alien investor must develop and direct the business operation or a function within the operation.

Job Shops

The greatest area of confusion surrounding Walsh and Pollard initially concerned the issue of the job shop. A job shop usually involves the providing of workers needed by an employer to perform predesignated duties. The employer often has position descriptions prepared for such workers. The positions to be filled by the workers are often positions that the employer cannot fill for a variety of reasons, such as unavailability of that type of worker or cost of locally hired workers. For example, a manufacturer needs 100 tool and die workers to meet its production schedule. If it has only 50 on staff, it might engage a job shopper to fill the other positions. The fact pattern of the Walsh and Pollard decision is not that of a job shop, nor does it in any way facilitate the creation of job shops under the E-2 visa classification. It is a pattern in direct contrast to a job shop, in which a business creating a new model required design engineering services that the business neither had the capacity to perform nor had any existing positions to fill in that regard. It is expectable, in such circumstances, that the business might contract with another business to provide the needed design for the model. The fact that the designing entity might prepare the design anywhere, even on the sites of the contracting business, does not alter the nature of the transaction. Since the distinction might be clouded in some circumstances, petitioners should exercise extreme care in filing such cases and not hesitate to submit any questionable cases for an advisory opinion.

EMPLOYER AND EMPLOYEE QUALIFICATIONS FOR E-1 AND E-2 VISAS

To qualify to bring an employee into the United States under an E Visa, the prospective employer in the United States must maintain immigration status under an E Visa. To qualify to bring an employee into the United States with an E visa, several criteria must be met:

1. The prospective employer must meet the nationality requirement. If the employer is an individual, he or she must be the nationality of the treaty country or, if the employer is a corporation or other business organization, at least 50 percent

of the ownership must have the nationality of the treaty country. A U.S. permanent resident alien does not qualify to bring in employees under E visas. Moreover, shares of a corporation or other business organization owned by permanent resident aliens cannot be considered in determining majority ownership by nationals of the treaty country to qualify the company for bringing in alien employees under an E visa.

2. The employer and the employee must have the same nationality; and

3. The employer, if not resident abroad, must be maintaining E status in the United States.

Executive and Supervisory Employee Responsibility

In substantiating the executive/supervisory element of the alien's job, the following factors must be addressed:

1. The title of the position to which the applicant is destined, its place in the firm's organizational structure, the duties of the position, the degree to which the applicant will have ultimate control and responsibility for the firm's overall operations or a major component thereof, the number and skill levels of the employees the applicant will supervise, the applicant's level of pay, and whether the applicant possesses qualifying executive or supervisory experience;

2. Whether the executive or supervisory element of the position is a principal and primary function and not an incidental or collateral function. For example, if the position principally requires management skills or entails key supervisory responsibility for a large portion of a firm's operations and only incidentally involves routine substantive staff work, an E classification would generally be appropriate. Conversely, if the position chiefly involves routine work and secondarily entails supervision of low-level employees, the position could not be termed executive or supervisory; and

3. The weight to be accorded a given factor; this may vary from case to case. For example, the position title of vice president or manager might be of use in assessing the supervisory nature of a position if the applicant were coming to a major operation with numerous employees. However, if the applicant were coming to a small two-person office, such a title in and of itself would be of little significance.

Essential Employees

The regulations provide E visa classification for employees who have special qualifications that make the service to be rendered essential to the efficient operation of the enterprise. The employee must, therefore, possess specialized skills, and similarly, such skills must be needed by the enterprise. The burden of proof to establish that the applicant has special qualifications essential to the effectiveness of the firm's U.S. operations is on the company and the applicant. The determination of whether an employee is an essential employee in this context requires the exercise of judgment. It cannot be decided by the mechanical application of a bright-line test. By its very nature, essentiality must be assessed on the particular facts in each case.

Duration of Essentiality

The applicant bears the burden of establishing, at the time of application, not only the need for the skills that he or she offers but also the length of time that such skills will be needed. In general, the E classification is intended for specialists and not for ordinary skilled workers. There are, however, exceptions to this generalization. Some skills may be essential for as long as the business is operating. Others, however, may be necessary for a shorter time, such as in start-up cases. Although there is a broad spectrum between the extremes set forth below, the petitioner may draw some perspective on this issue from the following examples:

1. Long-term need—The employer may show a need for the skill(s) on an ongoing basis when the employee(s) will be engaged in functions such as continuous development of product improvement, quality control, or provision of a service otherwise unavailable (as in Walsh and Pollard).

2. Short-term need—The employer may need the skills for only a relatively short (e.g., one or two years) period of time when the purpose of the employee(s) relates to start-up operations (of either the business or a new activity by the business) or to training and supervision of technicians employed in manufacturing, maintenance, and repair functions.

General Factors to Be Considered

Once the business has established the need for the specialized skills, the experience and training necessary to achieve such skills must be analyzed to recognize the special qualities of the skills in question. The question of duration of need will cause variances among the kinds of skills involved. The visa applicant must prove that he or she possesses these skills by demonstrating the requisite training and experience. In assessing the specialized skills and their essentiality, the petitioner should address such factors as the degree of proven expertise of the alien in the area of specialization, the uniqueness of the specific skills, the function of the job to which the alien is destined, and the salary such special expertise can command. In assessing the claimed duration of essentiality, the petitioning employer should take into account the period of training needed to perform the contemplated duties and, in some cases, the length of experience and training with the firm. The availability of U.S. workers provides another factor in assessing the degree of specialization the applicant possesses and the essentiality of this skilled worker to the successful operation of the business. This consideration is not a labor certification test, but a measure of the degree of specialization of the skills in question and the need for such. For example, a TV technician coming to train U.S. workers in new TV technology not generally available in the U.S. market probably would qualify for a visa. If the essential skills question cannot be resolved on the basis of initial documentation, the consular officer might ask the firm to provide statements from such sources as chambers of commerce, labor organizations, industry trade sources, or state employment services as to the unavailability of U.S. workers in the skill areas concerned. Using the criteria above, the petitioner can then make a judgment as to whether the employee is essential for the efficient operation of the enterprise for an indefinite period or for a shorter period. It might be determined that some skills are essential for as long as the business is operating. There may be little problem in assessing the need for the employee in the United States in the short term, such as start-up cases. Long-term employment presents a different issue, in that what is highly specialized and unique today might not be in a few years. It is anticipated that such changes would more likely occur in industries of rapid development, such as any computer-related industry. Although this may not be fully determinable at the time of initial application, the petitioner should monitor this at the time of any application for reissuance. The alien at that time will bear the burden of establishing that his or her specialized skills are still needed and that the applicant still possesses such skills.

Concept of Training

Essential employees possess skills that differentiate them from ordinarily skilled laborers. If an alien establishes that he or she has special qualifications and is essential for the efficient operation of the treaty enterprise for the long term, the training of U.S. workers is not an issue, since replacement workers are not required. In some cases, ordinarily skilled workers can qualify as essential employees, and almost always this involves workers needed for start-up or training purposes. A new business, or an established business expanding into a new field in the United States, might need employees who are ordinarily skilled workers for a short period of time. Such employees derive their essentiality from their familiarity with the overseas operations rather than the nature of their skills. The specialization of skills lies in the knowledge of the peculiarities of the operation of the employer's enterprise rather than in the rote skill held by the applicant. To avoid problems with subsequent applications, the petitioning employer should consider that at the time of the original application, it may be best to set a time frame within which the business must replace such foreign workers with locally hired employees.

Previous Employment with E Visa Firm

There is no requirement that an essential employee have a previous employment with the enterprise in question. The only time when such previous employment is a factor is when the needed skills can only be obtained by that employment. The focus of essentiality is on the business needs for the essential skills and of the alien's possession of such. Firms may need skills to operate their business, even though they do not have employees with such skills currently on their employment rolls.

INTENT TO DEPART UPON TERMINATION OF STATUS

An applicant for an E visa need not establish intent to proceed to the United States for a specific temporary period of time. In addition, an applicant for an E visa does not need to have a residence in a foreign country that he or she does not intend to abandon. The alien's expression of an unequivocal intent to return when the E status ends is normally sufficient, in the absence of specific indications that the alien's intent is to the contrary. If there are such objective indications, inquiry is justified to assess the applicant's true intent. An applicant might be a beneficiary of an immigrant visa petition filed on his or her behalf but might satisfy the consular officer that his or her intent is indeed to depart the United States upon termination of status and not stay in the United States to adjust status or otherwise remain in the United States regardless of legality of status.

NOTES

1. NAFTA Article 1601, Appendix 1603, § B(1)(a).
2. NAFTA Article 1601, Appendix 1603, § B(1)(b).
3. INA § 101(a)(15)(E).
4. INA § 101(a)(15)(E)(I).
5. Matter of, Int. Dec. #3111 (BIA 1988).

Chapter 4

Intracompany Transferees

Since 1970 the Immigration Act has allowed the temporary transfer of key executives of international companies to a branch or affiliate office in the United States. Rules that were made more restrictive in the 1980s were remedied in the 1990 Immigration Act, which created the present rules. In 1994, NAFTA introduced a shortened procedure for Canadian citizens entering as temporary intracompany transferees, but not for Mexican citizens, who must follow the standard procedure. These rules facilitate the movement into the United States of multinational company employees with special knowledge and expertise.

Under section 101(a)(15)(L) of the INA, an employee who within the preceding three years has been employed abroad for one continuous year by a qualifying organization may be admitted temporarily to the United States to be employed by a parent, branch, affiliate, or subsidiary of that employer in a managerial or executive capacity, or in a position requiring specialized knowledge. An employee transferred to the United States under this nonimmigrant classification is referred to as an intracompany transferee, and the organization that seeks the classification of an employee as an intracompany transferee is referred to as the petitioner. The visa issued is an L-1 visa.[1]

WHAT COMPANIES QUALIFY

The first requirement is that the company be a "Qualifying organization." This means a U.S. or foreign firm, corporation, or other legal entity that:

1. Exactly meets one of the qualifying relationships specified in the definitions of a parent, branch, affiliate, or subsidiary specified in the regulations;

2. Is or will be doing business as an employer in the United States, and in at least one other country, directly or through a parent, branch, affiliate, or subsidiary for the duration of the employee's stay in the United States as an intracompany transferee (engaging in international trade is not required); and

3. Otherwise meets the requirements of the act.

The qualifying relationships are all defined in the regulations. "Parent" means a firm, corporation, or other legal entity that has subsidiaries. "Branch" means an operating division or office of the same organization housed in a different location. "Subsidiary" means a firm, corporation, or other legal entity of which a parent owns, directly or indirectly, more than half of the entity and controls the entity; or owns, directly or indirectly, half of the entity and controls the entity; or owns, directly or indirectly, 50 percent of a 50–50 joint venture and has equal control and veto power over the entity; or owns, directly or indirectly, less than half of the entity, but in fact controls the entity. "Affiliate" means either one of two subsidiaries, both of which are owned and controlled by the same parent or individual; or one of two legal entities owned and controlled by the same group of individuals, each individual owning and controlling approximately the same share or proportion of each entity. In addition, if an affiliate is a partnership that is organized in the United States to provide accounting services along with managerial or consulting services and that markets its accounting services under an internationally recognized name under an agreement with a worldwide coordinating organization that is owned and controlled by the member accounting firms, a partnership (or similar organization) that is organized outside the United States to provide accounting services will be considered to be an affiliate of the U.S. partnership. To qualify it must market its accounting services under the same internationally recognized name under the agreement with the worldwide coordinating organization of which the United States partnership is also a member.

In addition, the qualifying organization must be "doing business," defined in the regulations as engaging in the regular, systematic, and continuous provision of goods or services. The mere presence of an agent or office of the qualifying organization does not constitute doing business.

Documentation must be provided with the petition to the INS that shows that the company is a qualifying organization, that it has a qualifying relationship, and that it is doing business. A document check list that companies may follow is set out in Appendix G.

QUALIFYING EMPLOYEES

The employee who is transferred to work in the U.S. company must qualify by the type of job held and the previous period of employment.

There is no educational requirement for the employee such as those for professional workers.

"Intracompany transferee" means an employee who, within three years preceding his or her application for admission into the United States, has been employed abroad continuously for one year by a firm or corporation or other legal entity, or parent, branch, affiliate, or subsidiary thereof, and who seeks to enter the United States temporarily in order to render his or her services to a branch of the same employer or a parent, affiliate, or subsidiary thereof in a capacity that is managerial, executive, or involves specialized knowledge. If the employee spends periods in the United States in a lawful status for a branch of the same employer, or a parent, affiliate, or subsidiary, or makes brief trips to the United States for business or pleasure, this time will not interrupt the one year of continuous employment abroad. However, these periods will not be counted toward fulfillment of the one year of continuous employment.

Managerial capacity means an assignment within an organization in which the employee primarily

1. Manages the organization, or a department, subdivision, function, or component of the organization;
2. Supervises and controls the work of other supervisory, professional, or managerial employees, or manages an essential function within the organization, or a department or subdivision of the organization;
3. Has the authority to hire and fire, or to recommend these actions, as well as other personnel actions (such as promotion and leave authorization) if another employee or other employees are directly supervised; if no other employee is directly supervised, functions at a senior level within the organizational hierarchy or with respect to the function managed; and
4. Exercises discretion over the day-to-day operations of the activity or function for which the employee has authority. A first-line supervisor is not considered to be acting in a managerial capacity merely by virtue of the supervisor's supervisory duties unless the employees supervised are professional.

"Executive capacity" means an assignment within an organization in which the employee primarily

1. Directs the management of the organization or a major component or function of the organization;
2. Establishes the goals and policies of the organization, component, or function;
3. Exercises wide latitude in discretionary decision making; and
4. Receives only general supervision or direction from higher-level executives, the board of directors, or stockholders of the organization.

"Specialized knowledge" means special knowledge possessed by an individual of the petitioning organization's product, service, research, equipment, techniques, management, or other interests, and its application in international markets, or an advanced level of knowledge or expertise in the organization's processes and procedures. A "specialized knowledge professional" means an individual who has specialized knowledge and is a member of the professions as defined in the INA.

PROCEDURE

There are two types of procedures. A U.S. organization may apply for one employee to be transferred and receive an L visa or may make a blanket petition that will allow, when approved, a number of employees to obtain L visas over a period of time under the same approval. In addition there are special procedures for citizens of Canada.

Individual Petitions

Individual petitions are filed to obtain L status for one individual. The U.S. organization, called the petitioner, must petition on an INS I-129 form. The petition must be accompanied by

1. Evidence that the petitioner and organization that employed or will employ the employee are qualifying organizations. This evidence can include documents that show common ownership, such as share certificate registers, joint venture agreements, or other such documents.

2. Evidence that the employee will be employed in an executive, managerial, or specialized knowledge capacity, including a detailed description of the services to be performed. This evidence generally includes a job description, organizational charts, and experience required for the job.

3. Evidence that the employee has at least one continuous year of full-time employment abroad with a qualifying organization within the three years preceding the filing of the petition. This may be a letter from the foreign business setting out the work history of the employee, personal tax returns showing income from the foreign business, copies of annual reports mentioning the employee in the qualifying occupation, and similar evidence.

4. Evidence that the employee's prior year of employment abroad was in a position that was managerial, executive, or involved specialized knowledge and that the employee's prior education, training, and employment qualifies him or her to perform the intended services in the United States. However, the work in the United States need not be the same work the employee performed abroad. This may be a letter from the foreign business describing the job duties, a job description from the foreign personnel manual, organizational chart, or annual report or other document showing the position of the employee.

5. If the petition indicates that the alien multinational executive who will be transferred is coming to the United States as a manager or executive to open, or to be employed in, a new office in the United States, the petitioner must submit evidence that sufficient physical premises to house the new office have been secured, that the beneficiary has been employed for one continuous year in the three-year period preceding the filing of the petition in an executive or managerial capacity, and that the proposed employment involves executive or managerial authority over the new operation. In addition to this, the petitioner must show that the intended U.S operation, within one year of the approval of the petition, will support an executive or managerial position. This is generally presented in a business plan that includes the proposed nature of the office, describing the scope of the entity, its organizational structure, and its financial goals; the size of the U.S. investment; the financial ability of the foreign entity to remunerate the beneficiary and commence doing business in the United States; and the organizational structure of the foreign entity.

6. If the petition indicates that the beneficiary is coming to the United States in a specialized knowledge capacity to open, or to be employed in, a new office, the petitioner must submit evidence that sufficient physical premises to house the new office have been secured, that the business entity in the United States is or will be a qualifying organization, and that the petitioner has the financial ability to remunerate the beneficiary and to commence doing business in the United States.

7. If the beneficiary is an owner or major stockholder of the company, the petition must be accompanied by evidence that the beneficiary's services are to be used for a temporary period and that the beneficiary will be transferred to an assignment abroad upon the completion of the temporary services in the United States.

8. Often the INS will request further information after reviewing the petition and supporting documentation.

Petitions to obtain L status are filed with the INS Service Center having jurisdiction over the place of employment for citizens of Mexico or at a northern port of entry for Canadian citizens.

Blanket Petitions

A business that meets certain requirements may file a blanket petition seeking continuing approval of itself and some or all of its parent, branches, subsidiaries, and affiliates as qualifying organizations. The requirements are

1. the petitioner and each of those entities are engaged in commercial trade or services;

2. the petitioner has an office in the United States that has been doing business for one year or more;

3. the petitioner has three or more domestic and foreign branches, subsidiaries, or affiliates; and

4. the petitioner and the other qualifying organizations have obtained approval of petitions for at least ten L managers, executives, or specialized knowledge professionals during the previous twelve months; or have U.S. subsidiaries or affiliates with combined annual sales of at least $25 million; or have a U.S. work force of at least 1,000 employees.

Managers, executives, and specialized knowledge professionals employed by firms, corporations, or other entities that have been found to be qualifying organizations pursuant to an approved blanket petition may be classified as intracompany transferees and admitted to the United States.

When applying for a blanket petition, the petitioner must include in the blanket petition all of its branches, subsidiaries, and affiliates that plan to seek to transfer employees to the United States under the blanket petition. An individual petition may be filed by the petitioner or organizations in lieu of using the blanket petition procedure. However, the petitioner and other qualifying organizations may not seek L classification for the same employee under both procedures, unless a consular officer first denies eligibility. Whenever a petitioner that has blanket L approval files an individual petition to seek L classification for a manager, executive, or specialized knowledge professional, the petitioner must advise the INS that it has blanket L approval and certify that the beneficiary has not and will not apply to a consular officer for L classification under the approved blanket petition.

A blanket petition is filed on form I-129 and must be accompanied by evidence that the petitioner meets the requirements of the law, and that all entities for which approval is sought are qualifying organizations. Any other evidence the INS deems necessary in the particular case must also be included.

Approval

Approval of an individual or a blanket petition is issued by the INS within 30 days after the date a completed petition has been filed. If the INS requests additional information from the petitioner, the 30-day processing period will begin again upon receipt of the information. An individual petition that is approved will be valid for the period of established need for the beneficiary's services, not exceeding three years, except where the beneficiary is coming to the United States to open, or to be employed in, a new office. If the beneficiary is coming to the United States to open, or to be employed in, a new office, the petition may be approved for a period not exceeding one year. An approved blanket petition is valid initially for a period of three years and may be extended indefinitely thereafter if the qualifying organizations have complied with the regulations.

Admission

If the employee beneficiary is in the United States at the time of filing and approval of the petition, his or her status will be changed to L-1, and the approval notice will include a new I-94 for the employee showing the expiration date of the L status.

A beneficiary who is outside the United States may apply for admission to the United States only while the individual or blanket petition is valid. The beneficiary of an individual petition will not be admitted for a date past the validity period of the individual petition. The beneficiary of a blanket petition may be admitted for three years even though the initial validity period of the blanket petition may expire before the end of the three-year period. If the blanket petition will expire while the employee is in the United States, the burden is on the petitioner to file for indefinite validity of the blanket petition or to file any individual petition in the employee's behalf to support the employee's status in the United States. The admission period for any beneficiary can not exceed three years unless an extension of stay is granted by the INS.

Limitation on Period of Stay

An employee who has spent five years in the United States in a specialized knowledge capacity, or seven years in the United States in a managerial or executive capacity in L-1 status,[2] may not be readmitted to the United States in L status unless he or she has resided and been physically outside the United States for the immediate prior year. If the emplyee makes brief visits to the United States for business and pleasure, he or she does not lose credit for the time already spent outside the United States. However, the time in the United States does not count toward fulfillment of the one-year requirement.

Extension of the Petition

Since initial L status is issued for less than three years, it may be extended to allow the employee to remain in that status for the maximum time. To extend an individual petition, the petitioner must file a petition extension on form I-129. Except for those petitions involving new offices, supporting documentation is not required, unless requested by the INS. A petition for an extension must be filed while the original L status is valid and the original petition has not expired.

A visa petition for an extension that involves the opening of a new office may be extended by filing a new form I-129, accompanied by the following:

1. Evidence that the U.S. and foreign entities are still qualifying organizations;

2. Evidence that the U.S. entity has been doing business for the previous year;

3. A statement of the duties performed by the beneficiary for the previous year and the duties the beneficiary will perform under the extended petition;

4. A statement describing the staffing of the new operation, including the number of employees and types of positions held, accompanied by evidence of wages paid to employees when the beneficiary will be employed in a managerial or executive capacity; and

5. Evidence of the financial status of the U.S. operation.

A blanket petition may only be extended indefinitely by filing a new form I-129 with a copy of the previous approval notice and a report of the transfer of employees in L status during the preceding three years. The report of transfers must include a list of the employees admitted under the blanket petition during the preceding three years, including positions held during that period, the employing entity, and the dates of initial admission and final departure date of each employee. The petitioner must state whether it still meets the criteria for filing a blanket petition and that it will document any changes in approved relationships and additional qualifying organizations.

If the petitioner in an approved blanket petition fails to request indefinite validity, or if indefinite validity, is denied, the petitioner and its other qualifying organizations must apply for L status for its employees it wants to transfer by filing individual petitions for the next three years. After that period the petitioner may seek approval of a new blanket petition.

Extension of Employee Status

In individual petitions, the petitioner must apply for the petition extension and the employee's extension of stay concurrently on form I-129. When the employee is a beneficiary under a blanket petition, a new certificate of eligibility, accompanied by a copy of the previous approved certificate of eligibility, must be filed by the petitioner to request an extension of the employee's stay. The petitioner must also request a petition extension. The start and end dates of extension must be the same for the petition and the beneficiary's extension of stay. The beneficiary must be physically present in the United States at the time the extension of stay is filed. If the employee is required to leave the United States for business or personal reasons while the extension requests are pending, the petitioner may request the INS to cable notification of approval of the petition extension to the consular office abroad where the employee will apply for a visa.

An extension of stay may be authorized in increments of up to two years for beneficiaries of individual and blanket petitions. The total period of stay may not exceed five years for employees employed in a specialized knowledge capacity. The total period of stay for an employee employed in a managerial or executive capacity may not exceed seven years. No further extensions can be granted. When an employee is initially admitted to the United States in a specialized knowledge capacity and is later promoted to a managerial or executive position, he or she must have been employed in the managerial or executive position for at least six months to be eligible for the total period of stay of seven years. The change to managerial or executive capacity must have been approved by the INS in an amended, new, or extended petition at the time that the change occurred.

Denial of Petition

When the INS makes an adverse decision because the petitioner did not submit sufficient supporting documentation, the INS will notify the petitioner of its intent to deny the petition and the basis for the denial. The petitioner will be granted a period of 30 days from the date of the notice in which to inspect and rebut the evidence. All relevant rebuttal material will be considered by the INS in making a final decision.

If an individual petition is denied, the petitioner will be notified of the denial, the reasons for the denial, and the right to appeal the denial within 30 days after the date a completed petition has been filed. If a blanket petition is denied in whole or in part, the petitioner will be notified within 30 days after the date a completed petition has been filed of the denial, the reasons for the denial, and the right to appeal the denial. If the blanket petition is denied in part, the INS will list those organizations that were found to qualify.

Revocation

The INS may revoke a petition at any time, even after the expiration of the petition. The approval of any individual or blanket petition is automatically revoked if the petitioner withdraws the petition or the petitioner fails to request indefinite validity of a blanket petition.

Revocation may also be made on notice. In such cases the INS will send to the petitioner a notice of intent to revoke the petition in relevant part if the INS finds that

1. One or more entities are no longer qualifying organizations;
2. The employee is no longer eligible;
3. A qualifying organization(s) violated requirements of the INS and the regulations;
4. The statement of facts contained in the petition was not true and correct;
5. Approval of the petition involved gross error; or

6. None of the qualifying organizations in a blanket petition have used the blanket petition procedure for three consecutive years.

The notice of intent to revoke will contain a detailed statement of the grounds for the revocation and the time period allowed for the revocation and the time period allowed for the petitioner's rebuttal. Upon receipt of this notice, the petitioner may submit evidence in rebuttal within 30 days of the notice. The INS will consider all relevant evidence presented in deciding whether to revoke the petition in whole or in part. If a blanket petition is revoked in part, the remainder of the petition will remain approved, and a revised approval notice will be sent to the petitioner with the revocation notice.

If an individual petition is revoked, the beneficiary is required to leave the United States, unless the beneficiary has obtained other work authorization from the INS. If a blanket petition is revoked, and the petitioner and beneficiaries already in the United States are otherwise eligible for L classification, the INS will extend the blanket petition for a period necessary to support the stay of those blanket L beneficiaries. No new beneficiaries may be classified or admitted under this limited extension.

Appeals

A petition denied in whole or in part may be appealed. A petition that has been revoked on notice in whole or in part may be appealed. However, automatic revocations may not be appealed.

Spouse and Children

The spouse and unmarried minor children of the beneficiary are entitled to L-2 nonimmigrant classification, subject to the same period of admission and limits as the beneficiary, if the spouse and unmarried minor children are accompanying or following to join the beneficiary in the United States. Neither the spouse nor any child may accept employment unless he or she has been granted their own employment authorization under an available nonimmigrant visa category.

Procedure for Canadian Citizens

United States businesses that want to transfer a Canadian employee to the U.S. office may follow the standard procedures set out above or may use special procedures created to comply with the terms of NAFTA. The special NAFTA rules are explained below.

Except for the filing of blanket petitions, a U.S. or foreign employer seeking to classify a citizen of Canada as an intracompany transferee may file an individual petition in duplicate on form I-129 in conjunction with an application for admission of the citizen of Canada. Such filing may be made with an immigration officer at a Class A port of entry located on the U.S.-Canada land border or at a U.S. pre-clearance/pre-flight station in Canada. The petitioning employer need not appear, but form I-129 must bear the authorized signature of the petitioner.

If a blanket petition has been approved, an immigration officer at a port of entry may determine the eligibility of individual citizens of Canada seeking L classification under an approved blanket petition. At these locations, citizens of Canada must present the original, and two copies of, the Intracompany Transferee Certificate of Eligibility prepared by the approved organization, as well as three copies of the notice of approval.

If a petition or certificate of eligibility submitted concurrently with an application for admission is lacking necessary supporting documentation or is otherwise deficient, the inspecting immigration officer will return it to the applicant so he or she can obtain the necessary documentation from the petitioner to overcome the deficiency. The fee to file the petition will be remitted when the documentary or other deficiency is overcome. If the petition or certificate of eligibility is clearly deniable, the immigration officer will accept the petition and the fee and notify the petitioner of the denial, the reasons for denial, and the right of appeal. If a formal denial order cannot be issued by the port of entry, the petition with a recommendation for denial will be forwarded to the appropriate INS Center for final action.

The Canadian citizen spouse and unmarried minor children of a Canadian citizen admitted in L status are entitled to the same nonimmigrant classification and same length of stay (including all limitations) as the principal employee. They are not required to present visas, and they will be admitted under the classification symbol L-2. Non-Canadian citizen spouses or unmarried minor children will be entitled to the same nonimmigrant classification and the same length of stay (including all limitations) as the principal, but they will be required to present a visa upon application for admission as L-2 unless otherwise exempt. The spouse and dependent minor children cannot accept employment in the United States unless otherwise authorized under the INA.

Labor Disputes

If the Secretary of Labor certifies to, or otherwise informs, the INS that a strike or other labor dispute involving a work stoppage of workers is in progress where the beneficiary is to be employed, and the temporary entry of the beneficiary may adversely affect the settlement of such labor dispute or the employment of any person who is involved in such dispute, a petition to classify a citizen of Mexico or Canada as an L-1 intracompany transferee may be denied. If a petition has already been approved, but the employee has not yet entered the United States, or has entered the United States but not yet commenced employment, the approval of the petition may be suspended, and an application for admission on the basis of the petition may be denied.

If there is a strike or other labor dispute involving a work stoppage of workers in progress, but such strike or other labor dispute is not certified, or the INS has not otherwise been informed by the Secretary of Labor that such a strike or labor dispute is in progress, the INS may not deny a petition or suspend an approved petition.

If the employee has already commenced employment in the United States under an approved petition and is participating in a strike or other labor dispute involving a work stoppage of workers, whether or not such strike or other labor dispute has been certified by the Department of Labor, the employee will not be deemed to be failing to maintain his or her status solely on account of past, present, or future participation in a strike or other labor dispute involving a work stoppage of workers but is subject to the following terms and conditions:

1. The employee will remain subject to all applicable provisions of the INA, and regulations promulgated in the same manner, as all other L nonimmigrants;

2. The status and authorized period of stay of such an employee is not modified or extended in any way by virtue of his or her participation in a strike or other labor dispute involving work stoppage of workers; and

3. Although participation by an L nonimmigrant employee in a strike or other labor dispute involving a work stoppage of workers will not constitute a ground for deportation, any employee who violates his or her status, or who remains in the United States after his or her authorized period of stay has expired, will be subject to deportation.

NOTES

1. 8 C.F.R. § 214.2(l)(1)(ii)(H).

2. This time limitation on stays also applies to H status or a combination of L and H status.

Part III

Professionals

Chapter 5

Categories of Professionals
Permitted under NAFTA

The U.S. immigration law recognizes professionals as a special category of workers who may obtain immigrant or nonimmigrant status. The definition of "professional" and the determination of who is a professsional for immigration purposes have been a matter of much statutory creation and amendments, regulation interpretation, litigation, and debate. Professionals have been defined based on education alone and the requirement of a university degree, by reference to listed occupations, by activities in specialized fields, by the requirement for specialized knowledge, by the requirements for state licensure, by the amount of responsibilities and decision making required in the job, or by requirement for extended periods of experience. New occupations have been added to the list of recognized professions, sometimes with great diffficulty involving negotiation, legislation, and litigation.

The drafters of NAFTA appeared to want to avoid the problem of defining who is a professional to facilitate the application for TN status. NAFTA[1] contains a list of 63 professions that are recognized as the only occupations that are professions for TN status. In addition to naming the professions, NAFTA sets out the exact requirements that a professional must document to prove he or she is a member of that profession. This makes it very easy for anyone to determine if he or she is a professional as defined by NAFTA and, as a result, makes the process of obtaining TN status more certain. On the other hand, the list of professionals cannot be changed to add new professional occupations that arise without a renegotiation of the treaty and agreement by all three Parties. In addition, a person who does not have the exact education or other requirements specified in NAFTA cannot be determined to be a professional and will not be able to obtain TN status.

REQUIREMENTS FOR PROFESSIONALS

The 63 professions are divided into categories of general, medical and allied professionals, scientists, and teachers. Thirty-nine professions require a degree only; fourteen require a degree or a state or provincial license; and seven can have either a degree or a diploma plus experience. Of the remaining three, one requires a degree plus training or experience; one, a degree or experience; and one, experience only. A state, provincial, or federal license means any document issued by, or under the authority of, a state, provincial, or federal government that permits a person to engage in regulated activity or profession. It does not include a license issued by a local government. Post-Secondary Diploma means a credential issued, on completion of two or more years of post-secondary education, by an academic institution in Canada or the United States. Post-Secondary Certificate means a certificate issued, on completion of two or more years of post-secondary education at an academic institution, by the federal government of Mexico or a state government in Mexico, an academic institution recognized by the Mexican federal government or a state government, or an academic institution created by federal or state law.

Proof of a degree is fairly simple since the professional will have the original and should provide a photocopy with the petition. There is no requirement for a four-year degree, and three-year degrees from Canada are acceptable. There is no requirement that transcripts be provided, but official transcripts would enhance the petition documentation, especially if the degree has a name that does not include the profession (e.g., B.S. with no mention of the scientific specialty), the institution awarding the degree is in a country other than Canada or Mexico, or the degree is from a less well-known institution. Proof of experience could take the form of letters from previous employers, letters from other professionals in the field who recognize the person as a professional, business records to show self-employment, published articles by and about the professional, memberships in professional organizations, and similar documentation.

If the profession requires a state or local license for an individual to fully perform the duties of that profession, the beneficiary for whom TN classification is sought must have that license prior to approval of the petition, and evidence of such licensing must accompany the petition. If a temporary license is available, and the beneficiary would be allowed to perform the duties of the profession without a permanent license, the INS will examine the nature of the duties, the level at which the duties are performed, the degree of supervision received, and any limitations that would be placed upon the beneficiary. If an analysis of the facts demonstrates that the beneficiary, although under supervision, would be fully authorized to perform the duties of the profession, TN classification may be granted. In certain professions that generally require licensure, a state may allow an individual to fully practice a profession under the supervision of licensed senior or supervisory personnel in that profession. In such cases, the INS will examine the nature of the duties and the level at which they are to be performed. If the facts demonstrate that the beneficiary, although under supervision, would fully perform the duties of the profession, TN classification may be granted.

Those professionals seeking admission with temporary licensure or without licensure should include in their petition package all relevant information and documentation that will support their case. This can include copies of state laws (statutes, regulations, and cases) that set out or support their position, a letter from the state licensing organization, details of the job and supervision, licenses held by the supervisor, and any variation in the job duties compared with those of someone fully licensed.

If the employee is a registered nurse, the prospective employer must submit evidence that the beneficiary has been granted a permanent state license, a temporary state license, or other temporary authorization issued by a State Board of Nursing, authorizing the beneficiary to work as a registered or graduate nurse in the state of intended employment in the United States.

All professionals, in addition to performing their profession, may perform training functions relating to the profession, including conducting seminars. The North American Free Trade Agreement does not allow a professional to become self-employed in his or her profession in the United States. However, a professional who is self-employed in Canada or Mexico may contract to provide prearranged services to a United States entity and obtain a TN status to enter the United States. to provide those services. All professionals must be employed by a qualified entity while they are in TN status.

PROFESSIONS

The following is a list of the professions listed in NAFTA for which TN status may be obtained. Each profession is listed with the education and experience requirements. The job description from the Dictionary of Occupational Titles[2] (DOT) is included with each occupation. This job description can be used by employers as a guide for drafting letters offering employment to ensure that the job offered comes within the scope of the DOT job descriptions.

GENERAL

Accountant

An accountant must have a Baccalaureate or Licenciatura Degree; or be a C.P.A., C.A., C.G.A., or C.M.A.

DOT: A term applied to an accountant who has met state legal requirements for public practice, and who has been certified by a state as possessing appropriate education and experience as evidenced by passing grade in nationally uniform Examination. Accountants, Certified Public may be employed by individual establishments, but usually provide a variety of accounting services to general public, either as an individual on a fee basis or as a member or salaried employee of firm which provides such services.

Architect

An architect must have a Baccalaureate or Licenciatura Degree; or state or provincial license.

DOT: Researches, plans, designs, and administers building projects for clients, applying knowledge of design, construction procedures, zoning and building codes, and building materials: Consults with client to determine functional and spatial requirements of new structure or renovation, and prepares information regarding design, specifications, materials, color, equipment, estimated costs, and construction time. Plans layout of project and integrates engineering elements into unified design for client review and approval. Prepares scale drawings and contract documents for building contractors. Represents client in obtaining bids and awarding construction contracts. Administers construction contracts and conducts periodic on-site observation of work during construction to monitor compliance with plans. May prepare operating and maintenance manuals, studies, and reports. May use computer-assisted design software and equipment to prepare project designs and plans. May direct activities of workers engaged in preparing drawings and specification documents.

Computer Systems Analyst

A computer systems analyst requires a Baccalaureate or Licenciatura Degree. An alternative way to be a member of this profession is to hold a Post-Secondary Diploma or a Post-Secondary Certificate and have three years experience in the profession.

DOT: Analyzes user requirements, procedures, and problems to automate processing or to improve existing computer system: Confers with personnel of organizational units involved to analyze current operational procedures, identify problems, and learn specific input and output requirements, such as forms of data input, how data is to be summarized, and formats for reports. Writes detailed description of user needs, program functions, and steps required to develop or modify computer program. Reviews computer system capabilities, workflow, and scheduling limitations to determine if requested program or program change is possible within existing system. Studies existing information processing systems to evaluate effectiveness and develops new systems to improve production or workflow as required. Prepares workflow charts and diagrams to specify in detail operations to be performed by equipment and computer programs and operations to be performed by personnel in system. Conducts studies pertaining to development of new information systems to meet current and projected needs. Plans and prepares technical reports, memoranda, and instructional manuals as documentation of program development. Upgrades system and corrects errors to maintain system after implementation. May assist computer programmer in resolution of work problems related to flow charts, project specifications, or programming. May prepare time and cost estimates for completing projects. May direct and coordinate work of others to develop, test, install, and modify programs.

Disaster Relief Insurance Claims Adjuster

A disaster relief claims adjuster employed by an insurance company located in the territory of a Party, or an independent claims adjuster, must have a Baccalaureate or Licenciatura Degree and must have successfully completed training in the appropriate areas of insurance adjustment pertaining to disaster relief claims. An alternate criterion to prove professional standing is to have three years experience in claims adjustment and successful completion of training in the appropriate areas of insurance adjustment pertaining to disaster relief claims.

DOT: No definition.

Economist

An economist must have a Baccalaureate or Licenciatura Degree.

DOT: Plans, designs, and conducts research to aid in interpretation of economic relationships and in solution of problems arising from production and distribution of goods and services: Studies economic and statistical data in area of specialization, such as finance, labor, or agriculture. Devises methods and procedures for collecting and processing data, utilizing knowledge of available sources of data and various econometric and sampling techniques. Compiles data relating to research area, such as employment, productivity, and wages and hours. Reviews and analyzes economic data in order to prepare reports detailing results of investigation, and to stay abreast of economic changes. Organizes data into report format and arranges for preparation of graphic illustrations of research findings. Formulates recommendations, policies, or plans to aid in market interpretation or solution of economic problems, such as recommending changes in methods of agricultural financing, domestic, and international monetary policies, or policies that regulate investment and transfer of capital. May supervise and assign work to staff. May testify at regulatory or legislative hearings to present recommendations. May specialize in specific economic area or commodity and be designated Agricultural Economist; Commodity-Industry Analyst; Financial Economist; Industrial Economist; International-Trade Economist; Labor Economist; Price Economist; Tax Economist.

Engineer

An engineer may have either a Baccalaureate or Licenciatura Degree or a state or provincial license. All fields of engineering are available for TN status.

DOT: A term applied to persons who possess educational qualifications, work experience, and legal certification where required as established by engineering schools, employers, and licensing authorities for employment in various fields of engineering. Engineers typically function in one or more activities, such as research, development, design, production, consulting, administration and management, teaching, technical writing, or technical sales and service. Classifications are made according to one or more engineering fields in which individual is qualified for employment, such as aeronautical, electrical, mechanical, chemical, mining, marine, or nuclear engineering.

Forester

A forester must have either a Baccalaureate or Licenciatura Degree or a state or provincial license.

DOT: Manages and develops forest lands and resources for economic and recreational purposes: Plans and directs forestation and reforestation projects. Maps forest areas, estimates standing timber and future growth, and manages timber sales. Plans cutting programs to assure continuous production of timber or to assist timber companies achieve production goals. Determines methods of cutting and removing timber with minimum waste and environmental damage and suggests methods of processing wood for various uses. Directs suppression of forest fires and conducts fire-prevention programs. Plans and directs construction and maintenance of recreation facilities, fire towers, trails, roads, and fire breaks. Assists in planning and implementing projects for control of floods, soil erosion, tree diseases, and insect pests in forests. Advises landowners on forestry management techniques and conducts public educational programs on forest care and conservation. May participate in environmental studies and prepare environmental reports. May supervise activities of other forestry workers. May patrol forests, enforce laws, and fight forest fires. May administer budgets. May conduct research to improve knowledge of forest management. May specialize in one aspect of forest management. May be designated Forestry Supervisor; Woods Manager.

Graphic Designer

Graphic designers can have either a Baccalaureate or Licenciatura Degree, or a Post-Secondary Diploma or Post-Secondary Certificate and three years experience.

DOT: Creates and designs graphic material for use as ornamentation, illustration, advertising, or cosmetic on manufactured materials and packaging: Receives assignment from customer or supervisor. Studies traditional, period, and contemporary design styles and motifs to obtain perspective. Reviews marketing trends and preferences of target and related markets. Integrates findings with personal interests, knowledge of design, and limitations presented by methods and materials. Creates, draws, modifies, and changes design to achieve desired effect. Confers with customer or supervisor regarding approval or desired changes to design. May be required to have specialized knowledge of material designed. May prepare original artwork and design model. May perform related duties, such as fabricating silk screens, drawing full-size patterns, or cutting stencils. May work with specific items, such as signs, packaging, wallpaper, ceramics, tile, glassware, monograms, crests, emblems, or embroidery.

Hotel Manager

A hotel manager must have a specialized degree and show a Baccalaureate or Licenciatura Degree in hotel/restaurant management. An alternative way to prove professional status is to have a Post-Secondary Diploma or Post-Secondary Certificate in hotel/restaurant management and three years experience in hotel or restaurant management.

DOT: Manages hotel or motel to ensure efficient and profitable operation: Establishes standards for personnel administration and performance, service to patrons, room rates, advertising, publicity, credit, food selection and service, and type of patronage to be solicited. Plans dining room, bar, and banquet operations. Allocates funds, authorizes expenditures, and assists in planning budgets for departments. Interviews, hires, and evaluates personnel. Answers patrons' complaints and resolves problems. Delegates authority and assigns responsibilities to department heads. Inspects guests' rooms, public access areas, and outside grounds for cleanliness and appearance. Processes reservations and adjusts guests' complaints when working in small motels or hotels.

Industrial Designer

An industrial designer requires a Baccalaureate or Licenciatura Degree or a Post-Secondary Diploma or Post-Secondary Certificate plus three years experience.

DOT: Originates and develops ideas to design the form of manufactured products: Reads publications, attends showings, and consults with engineering, marketing, production, and sales representatives to establish design concepts. Evaluates design ideas based on factors such as appealing appearance, design-function relationships, serviceability, materials and methods engineering, application, budget, price, production costs, methods of production, market characteristics, and client specifications. Integrates findings and concepts and sketches design ideas. Presents design to client or design committee and discusses need for modification and change. May design product packaging and graphics for advertising. May build simulated model, using hand and power tools and various materials. May prepare illustrations. May prepare or coordinate preparation of working drawings from sketches and design specifications. May design products for custom applications. May be required to have specialized product knowledge. Usually specializes in specific product or type of product including, but not limited to, hardware, motor vehicle exteriors and interiors, scientific instruments, industrial equipment, luggage, jewelry, housewares, toys, or novelties.

Interior Designer

An interior designer requires a Baccalaureate or Licenciatura Degree, or a Post-Secondary Diploma or Post-Secondary Certificate plus three years experience.

DOT: Plans, designs, and furnishes interior environments of residential, commercial, and industrial buildings: Confers with client to determine architectural preferences, purpose and function of environment, budget, types of construction, equipment to be installed, and other factors which affect planning interior environments. Integrates findings with knowledge of interior design and formulates environmental plan to be practical, esthetic, and conducive to intended purposes, such as raising productivity, selling merchandise, or improving life style of occupants. Advises client on interior design factors, such as space planning, layout and utilization of furnishings and equipment, color schemes, and color coordination. Renders design ideas in form of paste-ups, drawings, or illustrations, estimates material requirements and costs, and presents design to client for approval. Selects or designs and purchases furnishings, art works, and accessories. Subcontracts fabrication, installation, and arrangement of carpeting, fixtures, accessories, draperies, paint and wall coverings, art work, furniture, and related items. May plan and design interior environments for boats, planes, buses, trains, and other enclosed spaces. May specialize in particular field, style, or phase of interior design. May specialize in decorative aspects of interior design and be designated Interior Decorator.

Land Surveyor

A land surveyor requires either a Baccalaureate or Licenciatura Degree, or a state, provincial, or federal license.

DOT: Plans, organizes, and directs work of one or more survey parties engaged in surveying earth's surface to determine precise location and measurements of points, elevations, lines, areas, and contours for construction, mapmaking, land division, titles, mining, or other purposes: Researches previous survey evidence, maps, deeds, physical evidence, and other records to obtain data needed for surveys. Develops new data from photogrammetric records. Determines methods and procedures for establishing or reestablishing survey control. Keeps accurate notes, records, and sketches to describe and certify work performed. Coordinates findings with work of engineering and architectural personnel, clients, and others concerned with project. Assumes legal responsibility for work and is licensed by state.

Landscape Architect

A landscape architect requires a Baccalaureate or Licenciatura Degree. Transcripts showing course work would assist in showing a degree was related to landscape architecture.

DOT: Plans and designs development of land areas for projects, such as parks and other recreational facilities, airports, highways, and parkways, hospitals, schools, land subdivisions, and commercial, industrial, and residential sites: Confers with clients, engineering personnel, and architects on overall program. Compiles and analyzes data on such site conditions as geographic location; soil, vegetation, and rock features; drainage; and location of structures for preparation of environmental impact report and development of landscaping plans. Prepares site plans, working drawings, specifications, and cost estimates for land development, showing ground contours, vegetation, locations of structures, and such facilities as roads, walks, parking areas, fences, walls, and utilities, coordinating arrangement of existing and proposed land features and structures. Inspects construction work in progress to ensure compliance with landscape specifications, to approve quality of materials and work, and to advise client and construction personnel on landscape features. May be designated according to project as Highway-Landscape Architect; Park-Landscape Architect.

Lawyer

Lawyers include a Notary in the province of Quebec. They require a L.L.B., J.D., L.L.L., B.C.L., or Licenciatura degree (five years). An alternative is membership in a state or provincial bar. How a lawyer will practice the profession of law will be related to the individual's location and job. Many states require citizenship for admission to the bar, so a nonimmigrant lawyer in TN status clearly will not qualify and will be unable to practice law. Some states allow the registration of foreign legal counsel who will advise clients on the law in the province in which the lawyer is admitted to the bar. It is also possible for a lawyer to provide general legal counsel to one company on internal matters without becoming a member of the state bar; however, there are restrictions on the types of activities and procedures a person in this position can undertake. Lawyers can also accept teaching jobs and teach law courses.

DOT: Conducts criminal and civil lawsuits, draws up legal documents, advises clients as to legal rights, and practices other phases of law: Gathers evidence in divorce, civil, criminal, and other cases to formulate defense or to initiate legal action. Conducts research, interviews clients and witnesses, and handles other details in preparation for trial. Prepares legal briefs, develops strategy, arguments, and testimony in preparation for presentation of case. Files brief with court clerk. Represents client in court and before quasi-judicial or administrative agencies of government. Interprets laws, rulings, and regulations for individuals and businesses. May confer with colleagues with specialty in area of lawsuit to establish and verify basis for legal proceedings. May act as trustee, guardian, or executor. May draft wills, trusts, transfer of assets, gifts, and other documents. May advise corporate clients concerning transactions of business involving internal affairs, stockholders, directors, officers, and corporate relations with general public. May supervise and coordinate activities of subordinate legal personnel. May prepare business contracts, pay taxes, settle labor disputes, and administer other legal matters. May teach college courses in law. May specialize in specific phase of law.

Librarian

Librarians require an advanced degree: either a M.L.S., or a B.L.S. for which another Baccalaureate or Licenciatura Degree was a prerequisite.

DOT: Maintains library collections of books, serial publications, documents, audiovisual, and other materials, and assists groups and individuals in locating and obtaining materials: Furnishes information on library activities, facilities, rules, and services. Explains and assists in use of reference sources, such as card or book catalog or book and periodical indexes to locate information. Describes or demonstrates procedures for searching catalog files. Searches catalog files and shelves to locate information. Issues and receives materials for circulation or for use in library. Assembles and arranges displays of books and other library materials. Maintains reference and circulation materials. Answers correspondence on special reference subjects. May compile list of library materials according to subject or interests, using computer. May select, order, catalog, and classify materials. May prepare or assist in preparation of budget. May plan and direct or carry out special projects involving library promotion and outreach activity and be designated Outreach Librarian. May be designated according to specialized function as Circulation Librarian; Readers'-Advisory-Service Librarian; or Reference Librarian.

Management Consultant

A management consultant is one of the few professions that can have either a degree or experience. A Baccalaureate or a Licenciatura Degree is acceptable in the field. An alternative is equivalent professional experience as established by statement or professional credential attesting to five years experience as a management consultant, or five years experience in a field of specialty related to the consulting agreement.

Management consultants are generally not regular full-time employees, but this may be possible. They are usually independent consultants or employees of consulting firms that have a contract with a U.S. entity. If they are salaried employees they should be in supernumerary temporary positions.[3]   *DOT*: No DOT job description.[4]

Mathematician

Mathematicians include statisticians and require a Baccalaureate or Licenciatura Degree.

DOT: Conducts research in fundamental mathematics and in application of mathematical techniques to science, management, and other fields, and solves or directs solutions to problems in various fields by mathematical methods: Conducts research in such branches of mathematics as algebra, geometry, number theory, logic, and topology; and studies and tests hypotheses and alternative theories. Conceives and develops ideas for application of mathematics to wide variety of fields, including science, engineering, military planning, electronic data processing, and management. Applies mathematics or mathematical methods to solution of problems in research, development, production, logistics, and other functional areas, utilizing knowledge of subject or field to which applied, such as physics, engineering, astronomy, biology, economics, business and industrial management, or cryptography. Performs computations, applies methods of numerical analysis, and operates or directs operation of desk calculators and mechanical and electronic computation machines, analyzers, and plotters in solving problems in support of mathematical, scientific, or industrial research activity. Acts as advisor or consultant to research personnel concerning mathematical methods and applications. May be designated according to function as Mathematician, Applied; Mathematician, Research.

Range Manager/Range Conservationist

A range manager or range conservationist requires a Baccalaureate or Licenciatura Degree in the field.

DOT: Conducts research in range problems to provide sustained production of forage, livestock, and wildlife: Studies range lands to determine best grazing seasons and number and kind of livestock that can be most profitably grazed. Plans and directs construction and maintenance of range improvements, such as fencing, corrals, reservoirs for stock watering, and structures for soil-erosion control. Develops improved practices for range reseeding. Studies forage plants and their growth requirements to determine varieties best suited to particular range. Develops methods for controlling poisonous plants, and for protecting range from fire and rodent damage. May specialize in particular area and be designated Range Conservationist.

Research Assistant

Research assistants must be working in a post-secondary educational institution and hold a Baccalaureate or Licenciatura Degree. There is no requirement that the degree or area of research be in any specific field of study.

DOT: The DOT has a job description for graduate assistant (education). Assists department chairperson, faculty members or other professional staff members in college or university, by performing any combination of following duties: Assists in library, develops teaching materials, such as syllabi and visual aids, assists in laboratory or field research, prepares and gives examinations, assists in student conferences, grades examinations and papers, and teaches lower-level courses. May be designated by duties performed, or equipment operated.

Scientific Technician/Technologist

A scientific technician/technologist requires possession of (1) theoretical knowledge of any of the following disciplines: agricultural sciences, astronomy, biology, chemistry, engineering, forestry, geology, geophysics, meteorology, or physics; and (2) the ability to solve practical problems in any of those disciplines, or the ability to apply principles of any of those disciplines to basic or applied research. Evidence of the ability to solve practical problems or apply principles to research could include academic papers published and letters from former employers. A business person in this category must be seeking temporary entry for work in direct support of professionals in agricultural sciences, astronomy, biology, chemistry, engineering, forestry, geology, geophysics, meteorology, or physics.

DOT: No DOT job description.

Social Worker

A social worker requires a Baccalaureate or Licenciatura Degree.

DOT: A term applied to a worker performing social service functions, based on university-level education in social-welfare human services, or equivalency, in a public or voluntary social welfare agency, organization, or department, or in other settings, as in housing projects or in schools. Classifications are made according to work performed as Social Group Worker; Social Worker, Delinquency Prevention; Social Worker, Psychiatric. The DOT has complete job descriptions for the various specialties of social workers.

Sylviculturist

Sylviculturist includes a Forestry Specialist and requires a Baccalaureate or Licenciatura Degree.

DOT: Establishes and cares for forest stands: Manages tree nurseries and thins forests to encourage natural growth of sprouts or seedlings of desired varieties. Conducts research in such problems of forest propagation and culture as tree growth rate, effects of thinning on forest yield, duration of seed viability, and effects of fire and animal grazing on growth, seed production, and germination of different species. Develops techniques for measuring and identifying trees.

Technical Publications Writer

A technical publications writer can have either a Baccalaureate or Licenciatura Degree, or a Post-Secondary Diploma or Post-Secondary Certificate plus three years experience. Experience can be documented by letters from former employers or clients and copies of publications written by the professional.

DOT: Develops, writes, and edits material for reports, manuals, briefs, proposals, instruction books, catalogs, and related technical and administrative publications concerned with work methods and procedures, and installation, operation, and maintenance of machinery and other equipment: Receives assignment from supervisor. Observes production, developmental, and experimental activities to determine operating procedure and detail. Interviews production and engineering personnel and reads journals, reports, and other material to become familiar with product technologies and production methods. Reviews manufacturers' and trade catalogs, drawings and other data relative to operation, maintenance, and service of equipment. Studies blueprints, sketches, drawings, parts lists, specifications, mock-ups, and product samples to integrate and delineate technology, operating procedure, and production sequence and detail. Organizes material and completes writing assignment according to set standards regarding order, clarity, conciseness, style, and terminology. Reviews published materials and recommends revisions or changes in scope, format, content, and methods of reproduction and binding. May maintain records and files of work and revisions. May select photographs, drawings, sketches, diagrams, and charts to illustrate material. May assist in laying out material for publication. May arrange for typing, duplication, and distribution of material. May write speeches, articles, and public or employee relations releases. May edit, standardize, or make changes to material prepared by other writers or plant personnel and be designated Standard-Practice Analyst. May specialize in writing material regarding work methods and procedures and be designated Process-Description Writer.

Urban Planner

An urban planner includes a Geographer and requires a Baccalaureate or Licenciatura Degree.

DOT: Develops comprehensive plans and programs for utilization of land and physical facilities of cities, counties, and metropolitan areas: Compiles and analyzes data on economic, social, and physical factors affecting land use, and prepares or requisitions graphic and narrative reports on data. Confers with local authorities, civic leaders, social scientists, and land planning and development specialists to devise and recommend arrangements of land and physical facilities for residential, commercial, industrial, and community uses. Recommends governmental measures affecting land use, public utilities, community facilities, and housing and transportation to control and guide community development and renewal. May review and evaluate environmental impact reports applying to specified private and public planning projects and programs. When directing activities of planning department, is known as Chief Planner; Director, Planning. Usually employed by local government jurisdictions, but may work for any level of government, or private consulting firms.

Vocational Counselor

A vocational counselor requires a Baccalaureate or Licenciatura Degree.
DOT: No DOT job description.

MEDICAL/ALLIED PROFESSIONAL

Dentist

A dentist may have a D.D.S., D.M.D., Doctor en Odontologia or Doctor en Cirugia Dental or a state or provincial license.

DOT: Diagnoses and treats diseases, injuries, and malformations of teeth and gums, and related oral structures: Examines patient to determine nature of condition, utilizing x rays, dental instruments, and other diagnostic procedures. Cleans, fills, extracts, and replaces teeth, using rotary and hand instruments, dental appliances, medications, and surgical implements. Provides preventive dental services to patient, such as applications of fluoride and sealants to teeth, and education in oral and dental hygiene.

Dietitian

A dietitian requires a Baccalaureate or Licenciatura Degree or a state or provincial license.

DOT: Directs activities of institution department providing quantity food service and nutritional care: Administers, plans, and directs activities of department providing quantity food service. Establishes policies and procedures, and provides administrative direction for menu formulation, food preparation and service, purchasing, sanitation standards, safety practices, and personnel utilization. Selects professional dietetic staff, and directs departmental educational programs. Coordinates interdepartmental professional activities, and serves as consultant to management on matters pertaining to dietetics.

Medical Laboratory Technologist

A medical laboratory technologist in Canada is called a Medical Technologist in Mexico and the United States and must have either a Baccalaureate or Licenciatura Degree or a Post-Secondary Diploma or Post-Secondary Certificate and three years experience. A business person in this category must be seeking temporary entry to perform, in a laboratory, chemical, biological, hematological, immunologic, microscopic or bacteriological tests, and analyses for diagnosis, treatment, or prevention of diseases.

DOT: Performs medical laboratory tests, procedures, experiments, and analyses to provide data for diagnosis, treatment, and prevention of disease: Conducts chemical analyses of body fluids, such as blood, urine, and spinal fluid, to determine presence of normal and abnormal components. Studies blood cells, their numbers, and morphology, using microscopic technique.

Performs blood group, type, and compatibility tests for transfusion purposes. Analyzes test results and enters findings in computer. Engages in medical research under direction of Medical Technologist, Chief. May train and supervise students. May specialize in area such as hematology, bloodbank, serology, immunohematology, bacteriology, histology, or chemistry.

Nutritionist

A nutritionist must have a Baccalaureate or Licenciatura Degree in the field.
DOT: No DOT job description.[5]

Occupational Therapist

An occupational therapist must have a Baccalaureate or Licenciatura Degree or a state or provincial license.
DOT: Plans, organizes, and conducts occupational therapy program in hospital, institution, or community setting to facilitate development and rehabilitation of mentally, physically, or emotionally handicapped: Plans program involving activities, such as manual arts and crafts; practice in functional, prevocational, vocational, and homemaking skills, and activities of daily living; and participation in sensorimotor, educational, recreational, and social activities designed to help patients or handicapped persons develop or regain physical or mental functioning or adjust to handicaps. Consults with other members of rehabilitation team to select activity program consistent with needs and capabilities of individual and to coordinate occupational therapy with other therapeutic activities. Selects constructive activities suited to individual's physical capacity, intelligence level, and interest to upgrade individual to maximum independence, prepare individual for return to employment, assist in restoration of functions, and aid in adjustment to disability. Teaches individuals skills and techniques required for participation in activities and evaluates individual's progress. Designs and constructs special equipment for individual and suggests adaptation of individual's work-living environment. Requisitions supplies and equipment. Lays out materials for individual's use and cleans and repairs tools at end of sessions. May conduct training programs or participate in training medical and nursing students and other workers in occupational therapy techniques and objectives. May plan, direct, and coordinate occupational therapy program and be designated Director, Occupational Therapy.

Pharmacist

A pharmacist must have a Baccalaureate or Licenciatura Degree or a state or provincial license.

DOT: Compounds and dispenses prescribed medications, drugs, and other pharmaceuticals for patient care, according to professional standards and state and federal legal requirements: Reviews prescriptions issued by physician, or other authorized prescriber to assure accuracy and determine formulas and ingredients needed. Compounds medications, using standard formulas and processes, such as weighing, measuring, and mixing ingredients. Directs pharmacy workers engaged in mixing, packaging, and labeling pharmaceuticals. Answers questions and provides information to pharmacy customers on drug interactions, side effects, dosage, and storage of pharmaceuticals. Maintains established procedures concerning quality assurance, security of controlled substances, and disposal of hazardous waste drugs. Enters data, such as patient name, prescribed medication and cost, to maintain pharmacy files, charge system, and inventory. May assay medications to determine identity, purity, and strength. May instruct interns and other medical personnel on matters pertaining to pharmacy, or teach in college of pharmacy. May work in hospital pharmacy and be designated Pharmacist, Hospital.

Physician

Physicians require an M.D., Doctor en Medicina or a state or provincial license. A physician may only teach or undertake research. Even though possession of a license is proof of membership in the profession, physicians may not practice medicine or be involved in direct patient care while in TN status. However, patient care incidental to the physician's teaching or research is generally permissible.

DOT: The DOT has a job description for each specialty of physician.

Physiotherapist/Physical Therapist

A physiotherapist or physical therapist requires a Baccalaureate or Licenciatura Degree or a state or provincial license.

DOT: Plans and administers medically prescribed physical therapy treatment for patients suffering from injuries, or muscle, nerve, joint, and bone diseases, to restore function, relieve pain, and prevent disability: Reviews physician's referral (prescription) and patient's condition and medical records to determine physical therapy treatment required. Tests and measures patient's strength, motor development, sensory perception, functional capacity, and respiratory and circulatory efficiency, and records findings to develop or revise treatment programs. Plans and prepares written treatment program based on evaluation of patient data. Administers manual exercises to improve and maintain function. Instructs, motivates, and assists patient to perform various physical activities, such as nonmanual exercises, ambulatory functional activities, daily-living activities, and in use of assistant and supportive devices, such as crutches, canes, and prostheses. Administers treatments involving application of physical agents, using equipment, such as hydrotherapy tanks and whirlpool baths, moist packs, ultraviolet and infrared lamps, and ultrasound machines. Evaluates effects of treatment at various stages and adjusts treatments to achieve maximum benefit. Administers massage, applying knowledge of massage techniques and body physiology. Administers traction to relieve pain, using traction equipment. Records treatment, response, and progress in patient's chart or enters information into computer. Instructs patient and family in treatment procedures to be continued at home. Evaluates, fits, and adjusts prosthetic and orthotic devices and recommends modification to orthotist. Confers with physician and other practitioners to obtain additional patient information, suggests revisions in treatment program, and integrates physical therapy treatment with other aspects of patient's health care. Orients, instructs, and directs work activities of assistants, aides, and students. May plan and conduct lectures and training programs on physical therapy and related topics for medical staff, students, and community groups. May plan and develop physical therapy research programs and participate in conducting research. May write technical articles and reports for publications. May teach physical therapy techniques and procedures in educational institutions. May limit treatment to specific patient group or disability or specialize in conducting physical therapy research. In facilities where assistants are also employed, may primarily administer complex treatment, such as certain types of manual exercises and functional training, and monitor administration of other treatments. May plan, direct, and coordinate physical therapy program and be designated Director, Physical Therapy. Must comply with state requirement for licensure.

Psychologist

A psychologist requires a state or provincial license or a Licenciatura Degree.

DOT: This group includes occupations concerned with the collection, interpretation, and application of scientific data relating to human behavior and mental processes. Activities are in either applied fields of psychology or in basic science fields and research. The DOT has job descriptions for each specialty.

Recreational Therapist

A recreational therapist requires a Baccalaureate or Licenciatura Degree in the field.

DOT: Plans, organizes, and directs medically approved recreation program for patients in hospitals and other institutions: Directs and organizes such activities as sports, dramatics, games, and arts and crafts to assist patients to develop interpersonal relationships, to socialize effectively, and to develop confidence needed to participate in group activities. Regulates content of program in accordance with patients' capabilities, needs, and interests. Instructs patients in relaxation techniques, such as deep breathing, concentration, and other activities, to reduce stress and tension. Instructs patients in calisthenics, stretching and limbering exercises, and individual and group sports. Counsels and encourages patients to develop leisure activities. Organizes and coordinates special outings and accompanies patients on outings, such as ball games, sightseeing, or picnics to make patients aware of available recreational resources. Prepares progress charts and periodic reports for medical staff and other members of treatment team, reflecting patients' reactions and evidence of progress or regression. May supervise and conduct in-service training of other staff members, review their assessments and program goals, and consult with them on selected cases. May train groups of volunteers and students in techniques of recreation therapy. May serve as consultant to employers, educational institutions, and community health programs. May prepare and submit requisition for needed supplies.

Registered Nurse

A registered nurse requires a state or provincial license or a Licenciatura Degree.

DOT: Provides general medical care and treatment to patients in medical facility, such as clinic, health center, or public health agency, under direction of physician: Performs physical examinations and preventive health measures within prescribed guidelines and instructions of physician. Orders, interprets, and evaluates diagnostic tests to identify and assess patient's clinical problems and health care needs. Records physical findings, and formulates plan and prognosis, based on patient's condition. Discusses case with physician and other health professionals to prepare comprehensive patient care plan. Submits health care plan and goals of individual patients for periodic review and evaluation by physician. Prescribes or recommends drugs or other forms of treatment such as physical therapy, inhalation therapy, or related therapeutic procedures. May refer patients to physician for consultation or to specialized health resources for treatment. May be designated according to field of specialization as Pediatric Nurse Practitioner.

Veterinarian

A veterinarian requires a D.V.M., D.M.V., or Doctor en Veterinaria or a state or provincial license.

DOT: Diagnoses, and treats diseases and injuries of pets, such as dogs and cats, and farm animals, such as cattle or sheep: Examines animal to determine nature of disease or injury and treats animal surgically or medically. Tests dairy herds, horses, sheep, and other animals for diseases and inoculates animals against rabies, brucellosis, and other disorders. Advises animal owners about sanitary measures, feeding, and general care to promote health of animals. May engage in research, teaching, or production of commercial products. May specialize in prevention and control of communicable animal diseases and be designated Veterinarian, Public Health. May specialize in diagnosis and treatment of animal diseases, using roentgen rays and radioactive substances, and be designated Veterinary Radiologist.

SCIENTIST

Agriculturist

Agriculturist includes Agronomist and requires a Baccalaureate or Licenciatura Degree.

DOT: A term applied to persons with broad scientific knowledge of theoretical and actual agricultural practices and of livestock, such as varieties, breeds, feeding problems, and propagation of livestock; harvesting and marketing methods; and specialized areas of production. Provides technical and professional advice concerning agriculture to interested persons. Classifications are made according to specialty as Agronomist.

Animal Breeder

An animal breeder requires a Baccalaureate or Licenciatura Degree in the discipline.

DOT: Develops systems of breeding desirable characteristics, such as improvement in strength, maturity rate, disease resistance, and meat quality, into economically important animals: Determines generic composition of animal populations, and heritability of traits, utilizing principles of genetics. Crossbreeds animals within existing strains, or crosses strains to obtain new combinations of desirable characteristics. Selects progeny having desired strains of both parents, and continues process until acceptable result is obtained.

Animal Scientist

An animal scientist requires a Baccalaureate or Licenciatura Degree in the discipline.

DOT: Conducts research in selection, breeding, feeding, management, and marketing of beef and dual-purpose cattle, horses, mules, sheep, dogs, goats, and pet animals: Develops improved practices in feeding, housing, sanitation, and parasite and disease control. Controls breeding practices to improve strains of animals. May specialize in animal nutritional research and be designated Animal Nutritionist. May be designated according to animal specialty.

Apiculturist

An apiculturist requires a Baccalaureate or Licenciatura Degree in the discipline.

DOT: Studies bee culture and breeding: Conducts experiments regarding causes and controls of bee diseases and factors affecting yields of nectar and pollen on various plants visited by bees. Conducts research into various phases of pollination. Improves bee strains, utilizing selective breeding by artificial insemination.

Astronomer

An astronomer requires a Baccalaureate or Licenciatura Degree in the discipline.

DOT: Observes and interprets celestial phenomena and relates research to basic scientific knowledge or to practical problems, such as navigation: Studies celestial phenomena by means of optical, radio, or other telescopes, equipped with such devices as cameras, spectrometers, radiometers, photometers, and micrometers, which may either be on ground or carried above atmosphere with balloons, rockets, satellites, or space probes. Interprets information obtained in terms of basic physical laws. Determines sizes, shapes, brightness, spectra, and motions, and computes positions of sun, moon, planets, stars, nebulae, and galaxies. Calculates orbits of various celestial bodies. Determines exact time by celestial observations, and conducts research into relationships between time and space. Develops mathematical tables giving positions of sun, moon, planets, and stars at given times for use by air and sea navigators. Conducts research on statistical theory of motions of celestial bodies. Analyzes wave lengths of radiation from celestial bodies, as observed in all ranges of spectrum. Studies history, structure, extent, and evolution of stars, stellar systems, and universe. May design new and improved optical, mechanical, and electronics instruments for astronomical research. May specialize in either observational or theoretical aspects of stellar astronomy, stellar astrophysics, interstellar medium, galactic structure, extragalactic astronomy, or cosmology.

Biochemist

A biochemist requires a Baccalaureate or Licenciatura Degree in the discipline.

DOT: Studies chemical processes of living organisms: Conducts research to determine action of foods, drugs, serums, hormones, and other substances on tissues and vital processes of living organisms. Isolates, analyzes, and identifies hormones, vitamins, allergens, minerals, and enzymes and determines effects on body functions. Examines chemical aspects of formation of antibodies, and conducts research into chemistry of cells and blood corpuscles. Studies chemistry of living processes, antibodies, and conducts research into chemistry of cells and blood corpuscles. Studies chemistry of living processes, such as mechanisms of development of normal and abnormal cells, breathing and digestion, and of living energy changes, such as growth, aging, and death. May specialize in particular area or field of work and be designated Chemist, Clinical; Chemist, Enzymes; Chemist, Proteins; Chemist, Steroids. May clean, purify, refine, and otherwise prepare pharmaceutical compounds for commercial distribution and develop new drugs and medications and be designated Chemist, Pharmaceutical.

Biologist

A biologist requires a Baccalaureate or Licenciatura Degree in the discipline.

DOT: Studies basic principles of plant and animal life, such as origin, relationship, development, anatomy, and functions: May collect and analyze biological data to determine environmental effects of present and potential use of land and water areas, record data, and inform public, state, and federal representatives regarding test results. May prepare environmental impact reports. May specialize in research centering around particular plant, animal, or aspect of biology. May teach. May specialize in wildlife research and management and be designated Wildlife Biologist.

Chemist

A chemist requires a Baccalaureate or Licenciatura Degree in the discipline.

DOT: Conducts research, analysis, synthesis, and experimentation on substances, for such purposes as product and process development and application, quantitative and qualitative analysis, and improvement of analytical methodologies: Devises new equipment, and develops formulas, processes, and methods for solution of technical problems. Analyzes organic and inorganic compounds to determine chemical and physical properties, utilizing such techniques as chromatography, spectroscopy, and spectrophotometry. Induces changes in composition of substances by introduction of heat, light, energy, and chemical catalysts. Conducts research on manufactured products to develop and improve products. Conducts research into composition, structure, properties, relationships, and reactions of matter. Confers with scientists and engineers regarding research, and prepares technical papers and reports. Prepares standards and specifications for processes, facilities, products, and tests. May be designated according to chemistry specialty as Chemist, Analytical; Chemist, Inorganic; Chemist, Organic; Chemist, Physical.

Dairy Scientist

A dairy scientist requires a Baccalaureate or Licenciatura Degree in the discipline.

DOT: Conducts research in selection, breeding, feeding, and management of dairy cattle: Studies feed requirements of dairy animals and nutritive value of feed materials. Carries out experiments to determine effects of different kinds of feed and environmental conditions on quantity, quality, and nutritive value of milk produced. Develops improved practices in care and management of dairy herds and use of improved buildings and equipment. Studies physiology of reproduction and lactation, and carries out breeding programs to improve dairy breeds. May be designated according to specialty as Dairy-Management Specialist; Dairy-Nutrition Specialist.

Entomologist

An entomologist requires a Baccalaureate or Licenciatura Degree in the discipline.

DOT: Studies insects and their relation to plant and animal life: Identifies and classifies species of insects and allied forms, such as mites and spiders. Aids in control and elimination of agricultural, structural, and forest pests by developing new and improved pesticides and cultural and biological methods, including use of natural enemies of pests. Studies insect distribution and habitat and recommends methods to prevent importation and spread of injurious species.

Epidemiologist

An epidemiologist requires a Baccalaureate or Licenciatura Degree in the discipline.

DOT: Plans, directs, and conducts studies concerned with incidence of disease in industrial settings and effects of industrial chemicals on health: Confers with industry representatives to select occupational groups for study and to arrange for collection of data concerning work history of individuals and disease concentration and mortality rates among groups. Plans methods of conducting epidemiological studies and provides detailed specifications for collecting data to personnel participating in studies. Develops codes to facilitate computer input of demographic and epidemiological data for use by data processing personnel engaged in programming epidemiological statistics. Compares statistics on causes of death among members of selected working populations with those among general population, using life-table analyses. Analyzes data collected to determine probable effects of work settings and activities on disease and mortality rates, using valid statistical techniques and knowledge of epidemiology. Presents data in designated statistical format to illustrate common patterns among workers in selected occupations. Initiates and maintains contacts with statistical and data processing managers in other agencies to maintain access to epidemiological source materials. Evaluates materials from all sources for addition to or amendment of epidemiological data bank. Plans and directs activities of clerical and statistical personnel engaged in tabulation and analysis of epidemiological information to ensure accomplishment of objectives.

Geneticist

A geneticist requires a Baccalaureate or Licenciatura Degree in the discipline.

DOT: Studies inheritance and variation of characteristics in forms of life: Performs experiments to determine laws, mechanisms, and environmental factors in origin, transmission, and development of inherited traits. Analyzes determinants responsible for specific inherited traits, such as color differences, size, and disease resistance to improve or to understand relationship of heredity to maturity, fertility, or other factors. Devises methods for altering or producing new traits, making use of chemicals, heat, light, or other means. May specialize in particular branch of genetics, such as molecular genetics or population genetics. May perform human genetic counseling or medical genetics.

Geologist

A geologist requires a Baccalaureate or Licenciatura Degree in the discipline.

DOT: Studies composition, structure, and history of earth's crust: Examines rocks, minerals, and fossil remains to identify and determine sequence of processes affecting development of earth. Applies knowledge of chemistry, physics, biology, and mathematics to explain these phenomena and to help locate mineral, geothermal, and petroleum deposits and underground water resources. Studies ocean bottom. Applies geological knowledge to engineering problems encountered in construction projects, such as dams, tunnels, and large buildings. Studies fossil plants and animals to determine their evolutionary sequence and age. Prepares geologic reports and maps, interprets research data, and recommends further study or action. May specialize in area of study and be designated Geomorphologist; Oceanographer, Geological; Photogeologist. May conduct or participate in environmental studies and prepare environmental reports. Workers applying principles of rock and soil mechanics for engineering projects may be designated Geological Engineer. Workers applying all branches of geologic knowledge to conditions that affect planning, design, construction, operation, and safety to engineering projects may be designated Engineering Geologist.

Geochemist

A geochemist requires a Baccalaureate or Licenciatura Degree in the discipline.

DOT: No DOT job description.

Geophysicist

A geophysicist, which includes an Oceanographer in Mexico and the United States, requires a Baccalaureate or Licenciatura Degree in the discipline.

DOT: Studies physical aspects of earth, including its atmosphere and hydrosphere: Investigates and measures seismic, gravitational, electrical, thermal, and magnetic forces affecting earth, utilizing principles of physics, mathematics, and chemistry. Analyzes data obtained to compute shape of earth, estimate composition and structure of earth's interior, determine flow pattern of ocean tides and currents, study physical properties of atmosphere, and help locate petroleum and mineral deposits. Investigates origin and activity of glaciers, volcanoes, and earthquakes. Compiles data to prepare navigational charts and maps, predict atmospheric conditions, prepare environmental reports, and establish water supply and flood-control programs. May study specific aspect of geophysics and be designated Geomagnetician; Glaciologist; Oceanographer, Physical; Tectonophysicist; Volcanologist.

Horticulturist

A horticulturist requires a Baccalaureate or Licenciatura Degree in the discipline.

DOT: Conducts experiments and investigations to determine methods of breeding, producing, storing, processing, and transporting of fruits, nuts, berries, vegetables, flowers, bushes, and trees: Experiments to develop new or improved varieties having higher yield, quality, nutritional value, resistance to disease, or adaptability to climates, soils, uses, or processes. Determines best methods of planting, spraying, cultivating, and harvesting. May specialize in research, breeding, production, or shipping and storage of fruits, nuts, berries, vegetables, ornamental plants, or other horticultural products and be identified according to specialty. May prepare articles and give lectures on horticultural specialty.

Meteorologist

A meteorologist requires a Baccalaureate or Licenciatura Degree in the discipline.

DOT: Analyzes and interprets meteorological data gathered by surface and upper-air stations, satellites, and radar to prepare reports and forecasts for public and other users: Studies and interprets synoptic reports, maps, photographs, and prognostic charts to predict long and short range weather conditions. Operates computer graphic equipment to produce weather reports and maps for analysis, distribution to users, or for use in televised weather broadcast. Issues hurricane and other severe weather warnings. May broadcast weather forecast over television or radio. May prepare special forecasts and briefings for particular audiences, such as those involved in air and sea transportation, agriculture, fire prevention, air-pollution control, and school groups. May direct forecasting services at weather station, or at radio or television broadcasting facility. May conduct basic or applied research in meteorology. May establish and staff weather observation stations.

Pharmacologist

A pharmacologist requires a Baccalaureate or Licenciatura Degree in the discipline.

DOT: Studies effects of drugs, gases, dusts, and other materials on tissue and physiological processes of animals and human beings: Experiments with animals, such as rats, guinea pigs, and mice, to determine reactions of drugs and other substances on functioning of organs and tissues, noting effects on circulation, respiration, digestion, or other vital processes. Standardizes drug dosages or methods of immunizing against industrial diseases by correlating results of animal experiments with results obtained from clinical experimentation on human beings. Investigates preventative methods and remedies for diseases, such as silicosis and lead, mercury, and ammonia poisoning. Analyzes food preservatives and colorings, vermin poisons, and other materials to determine toxic or nontoxic properties. Standardizes procedures for manufacture of drugs and medicinal compounds.

Physicist

A physicist, which includes an Oceanographer in Canada, requires a Baccalaureate or Licenciatura Degree in the discipline.

DOT: Conducts research into phases of physical phenomena, develops theories and laws on basis of observation and experiments, and devises methods to apply laws and theories of physics to industry, medicine, and other fields: Performs experiments with masers, lasers, cyclotrons, betatrons, telescopes, mass spectrometers, electron microscopes, and other equipment to observe structure and properties of matter, transformation and propagation of energy, relationships between matter and energy, and other physical phenomena. Describes and expresses observations and conclusions in mathematical terms. Devises procedures for physical testing of materials. Conducts instrumental analyses to determine physical properties of materials. May specialize in one or more branches of physics and be designated Physicist, Acoustics; Physicist, Astrophysics; Physicist, Atomic, Electronic And Molecular; Physicist, Cryogenics; Physicist, Electricity And Magnetism; Physicist, Fluids. May be designated: Physicist, Light and Optics; Physicist, Nuclear; Physicist, Plasma; Physicist, Solid Earth; Physicist, Solid State; Physicist, Thermodynamics.

Plant Breeder

A plant breeder requires a Baccalaureate or Licenciatura Degree in the discipline.

DOT: Plans and carries out breeding studies to develop and improve varieties of crops: Improves specific characteristics, such as yield, size, quality, maturity, and resistance to frost, drought, disease and insect pests in plants, utilizing principles of genetics and knowledge of plant growth. Develops variety and selects most desirable plants for crossing. Breeds plants, using methods such as inbreeding, crossbreeding, backcrossing, outcrossing, mutating, or interspecific hybridization and selection. Selects progeny having desired characteristics and continues breeding and selection process to reach desired objectives.

Poultry Scientist

A poultry scientist requires a Baccalaureate or Licenciatura Degree in the discipline.

DOT: Conducts research in breeding, feeding, and management of poultry: Examines selection and breeding practices to increase efficiency of production and improve quality of poultry products. Studies nutritional requirements of various classes of poultry. Develops improved practices in incubation, brooding, feeding, rearing, housing, artificial insemination, and disease and parasite prevention and control. Studies effects of management practices and processing methods on quality of eggs and other poultry products. May specialize in artificial insemination.

Soil Scientist

A soil scientist requires a Baccalaureate or Licenciatura Degree in the discipline.

DOT: Studies soil characteristics and maps soil types, and investigates responses of soils to known management practices to determine use capabilities of soils and effects of alternative practices on soil productivity: Classifies soils according to standard types. Conducts experiments on farms or experimental stations to determine best soil types for different plants. Performs chemical analysis on micro-organism content of soil to determine microbial reactions and chemical and mineralogical relationship to plant growth. Investigates responses of specific soil types to tillage, fertilization, nutrient transformations, crop rotation, environmental consequences, water, gas or heat flow, industrial waste control and other soil management practices. Advises interested persons on rural or urban land use. May specialize in one or more types of activities relative to soil management and productivity and be designated Soil Fertility Expert.

Zoologist

A zoologist requires a Baccalaureate or Licenciatura Degree in the discipline.

DOT: Studies origin, interrelationships, classification, life histories, habits, life processes, diseases, relation to environment, growth and development, genetics, and distribution of animals: Studies animals in natural habitat and collects specimens for laboratory study. Dissects and examines specimens under microscope and uses chemicals and various types of scientific equipment to carry out experimental studies. Prepares collections of preserved specimens or microscopic slides for such purposes as identification of species, study of species development, and study of animal diseases. May raise specimens for experimental purposes. May specialize in one aspect of animal study, such as functioning of animal as an organism, or development of organism from egg to embryo stage. May specialize in study of reptiles, frogs, and salamanders and be designated Herpetologist; of fish and fishlike forms and be designated Ichthyologist; of sponges, jellyfish, and protozoa and be designated Invertebrate Zoologist; of birds and be designated Ornithologist; of mammals and be designated Mammalogist. May study animals for purposes of identification and classification and be designated Animal Taxonomist; or study effects of environment on animals and be designated Animal Ecologist.

TEACHERS

Only three types of teachers qualify under NAFTA: college, seminary, and university. Each requires a Baccalaureate or Licenciatura Degree. The INA in its definition of professional (for other visa categories) also includes elementary school and secondary school teachers and academics. NAFTA reduced the categories for teachers to only postsecondary institutions. In doing so, it eliminated the problems that might be associated with obtaining a state teaching license, which generally is required only for elementary and secondary schools, not for post-secondary institutions.

DOT: Conducts college or university courses for undergraduate or graduate students: Teaches one or more subjects, such as economics, chemistry, law, or medicine, within prescribed curriculum. Prepares and delivers lectures to students. Compiles bibliographies of specialized materials for outside reading assignments. Stimulates class discussions. Compiles, administers, and grades examinations, or assigns this work to others. Directs research of other teachers or graduate students working for advanced academic degrees. Conducts research in particular field of knowledge and publishes findings in professional journals. Performs related duties, such as advising students on academic and vocational curricula, and acting as adviser to student organizations. Serves on faculty committee providing professional consulting services to government and industry. May be designated according to faculty rank in traditional hierarchy as determined by institution's estimate of scholarly maturity as Associate Professor; Professor; or according to rank distinguished by duties assigned or amount of time devoted to academic work as Research Assistant; Visiting Professor. May teach in two-year college and be designated Teacher, Junior College; or in technical institute and be designated Faculty Member, Technical Institute. May be designated: Acting Professor; Assistant Professor; Clinical Instructor; Instructor; Lecturer; Teaching Assistant.

NOTES

1. Appendix 1603.D.1 to Annex 1603.
2. U.S. Department of Labor, Employment and Training Administration, 1991.
3. 67 Interpreter Releases 639–40, June 4, 1990.
4. The DOT index does include the term "consultant," but the listing, 199.251-010, is for Tester, Food Products (any industry), alternate title consultant. This does not relate to the profession of Management Consultant.
5. The DOT index has two references under the term "nutritionist." The first, 096.121-014, is for the occupation of Home Economist. The second, 077.127-010, is:

COMMUNITY DIETITIAN Plans, organizes, coordinates, and evaluates nutritional component of health care services for organization: Develops and implements plan of care based on assessment of nutritional needs and available sources and correlates plan with other health care. Evaluates nutritional care and provides followup continuity of care. Instructs individuals and families in nutritional principles, diet, food selection, and economics and adapts teaching plans to individual life style. Provides consultation to and works with community groups. Conducts or participates in in-service education and consultation with professional staff and supporting personnel of own and related organizations. Plans or participates in development of program proposals for funding. Plans, conducts, and evaluates dietary studies and participates in nutritional and epidemiologic studies with nutritional component. Evaluates food service systems and makes recommendation for conformance level that will provide optional nutrition and quality food if associated with group care institutions. May be employed by public health agency and be designated Nutritionist, Public Health.

Chapter 6

Procedures for Admission to the United States

The procedure for admission of professionals is different for Canadian citizens and Mexican citizens. There is a very simplified procedure available for Canadian citizen professionals and one that includes more requirements for Mexican citizen professionals.

PROCEDURE FOR PROFESSIONAL CITIZENS OF CANADA

The procedure for an initial application for TN status for Canadian citizen professionals is fast, basic, and relatively inexpensive. There is no requirement for labor certification or a prior petition being filed with the INS. A Canadian citizen who is one of the listed professionals under NAFTA applies for admission to the United States in TN status by appearing with the required documents and making an application in person at a Class A port of entry, at a U.S. airport handling international traffic, or at a U.S. pre-clearance/pre-flight station.[1] The applicant appears in person, and the employer does not need to appear. The matter is adjudicated on the spot by the free trade officer. Generally the applicant does not need to make an appointment but merely needs to appear during the hours that a free trade officer is on duty.

Documentation Required

A Canadian citizen seeking admission as a TN nonimmigrant does not require a visa but is required to present the following documents:

1. Proof of Canadian citizenship. Unless the Canadian is traveling from outside the Western hemisphere, no passport is required. However, an applicant for admis-

sion must establish Canadian citizenship by showing a birth certificate, certificate of naturalization, or a passport.

2. Documentation demonstrating engagement in business activities at a professional level and demonstrating professional qualifications. The applicant must present sufficient documentation to satisfy the immigration officer at the time of application for admission that the applicant is seeking entry to the United States to engage in business activities for a U.S. employer or entity at a professional level, and that the applicant meets the criteria to perform at such a professional level. This documentation may be in the form of a letter from the prospective employer in the United States or from the foreign employer, in the case of a Canadian citizen seeking entry to provide prearranged services to a U.S. entity. This documentation may be required to be supported by licenses, diplomas, degrees, certificates, or membership in a professional organization. Degrees, diplomas, or certificates received by the applicant from an educational institution not located within Canada, Mexico, or the United States must be accompanied by an evaluation by a reliable credentials evaluation service that specializes in evaluating foreign educational credentials.

The documentation must clearly show

1. The profession of the applicant is one specified in NAFTA;

2. The professional activities, including a brief summary of daily job duties, if appropriate, that the applicant will engage in for the U.S. employer or entity;

3. The anticipated length of stay;

4. The educational qualifications or appropriate credentials which demonstrate that the Canadian citizen has professional-level status;

5. The arrangements for remuneration for services to be rendered; and

6. If required by state or local law, the compliance of the Canadian citizen with all applicable laws and licensing requirements for the professional activity in which he or she will be engaged.

The documentation should include a letter from the U.S. employer that sets out the Canadian citizen's profession and its licensing requirements, professional activities and job duties, remuneration, and length of stay. The applicant should take originals of degrees, diplomas, and licenses, and a good photocopy of each, to give to the INS free trade officer. Any documents that are not in English must have an English language translation that is certified by the translator as to its accuracy. If there is no license requirement for an occupation that generally requires a license, for example lawyers or teachers, the applicant should take sufficient documentation to fully show there is no licensing requirement for the particular job. This may include a photocopy of statutes, a letter from the licensing organization, and a letter from the employer.

Admission

Once the INS officer reviews the documentation and determines that the Canadian citizen qualifies for admission, the officer will prepare and present an INS form I-94 to the professional. The I-94 will include the classification symbol TN and will be valid for a period of up to one year, indicated by the issue and expiry date written on the front of the document. The INS officer will put the legend "multiple entry" on the form I-94 and this will allow the professional to leave and reenter the United States during the authorized period of stay. On the reverse of the I-94, the INS officer will write the profession and the name and address of the employer. The Canadian may only be employed by the employer on the back of the I-94.

Upon payment of the required fee of $50, the INS officer will give the applicant an official fee receipt.

The approval procedure generally takes less than half an hour. The TN status will commence the day of the approval; and the Canadian citizen professional, if he or she is prepared to do so, may proceed into the United States and start employment.

PROCEDURE FOR MEXICAN CITIZEN PROFESSIONAL

The procedure for a Mexican citizen is the same as that for nurses seeking an H-1A visa and other professionals seeking an H-1B visa.[2] The procedure requires three steps:

1. Obtaining a labor condition from the Department of Labor,
2. Obtaining an approval notice on a form I-129 petition, and
3. Obtaining the TN visa at a U.S. consulate in Mexico.

The first two steps are performed by the U.S. employer, and the third step is done by the Mexican citizen professional. The whole procedure generally takes between three to four months to complete.

Labor Condition

Obtaining a labor condition involves two steps. First, the employer must request a prevailing wage from the state Department of Labor (DOL) where the Mexican citizen professional will be working. Each DOL has a form that must be used to request the prevailing wage. Information required to complete the form includes the name and address of the employer, the city where the employee will be working, the wages offered, the job title, a job description, and the name of the potential employee. Other information may be required by some states. Generally, employers may fax the completed form to the DOL. A prevailing wage will be faxed or mailed to the employer within a few days or weeks depending on the state. An employer must pay at least 95 percent of the prevailing wage to the employee.

After obtaining the prevailing wage, the employer must complete a form ETA 9029 for a nurse and ETA 9035 for all other professionals. These forms are called Labor Condition Applications (LCAs). They require the full legal name of the employer, the federal employer identification number, and the employer's phone and fax number and complete address. They also require the job title, if the job is full- or part-time, the rate of pay to be paid to the employee, the prevailing wage, the start and end date of the temporary employment (not to exceed one year), and the city and state where the employee will work. The forms also require a three-digit occupational group code from a list supplied with the instructions for completing the form.

The employer must also check four statements printed on the form that the employee will be paid the prevailing wage, that the employment will not adversely affect the working conditions of workers similarly employed, that there is not a strike or lockout on the date the application is signed and submitted, and that a copy of the application has been provided to any bargaining representative (if any) or was posted for at least ten days in two conspicuous locations at the workplace.

The employer must sign and date the labor condition application and fax two copies to the office of Employment and Training Administration responsible for approving such applications. An approved LCA will be mailed to the employer within two to four weeks.

The Petition to INS

A U.S. employer seeking to classify a citizen of Mexico as a TN professional temporary employee may file a petition on form I-129, "Petition for Nonimmigrant Worker," and all supporting documentation with the Northern Service Center.[3] This procedure must be followed even in emergent circumstances. The petitioner may submit a legible photocopy of a document in support of the visa petition in lieu of the original document. The original document should be available in the event that the INS requests it.

Completing the I-129

The employer completes and signs the form I-129. It is important that every part of the form be completed; information can be typed or printed in black ink. If a question or information box does not apply to the employer or the employee, the employer should indicate this by putting "N/A" in the space provided.

To allow the service center time to process the petition, it should be filed at least 45 days, but not more than four months, before the new employment is to begin. The employee will not be able to start the new job until an approval notice is received from INS. Employers should also allow time for the Mexican citizen to receive the approval notice from the employer and to visit a U.S. consulate to receive his or her visa.

Part 1 of the form requires the employer's name, address, and IRS Tax Identification number. The employer will complete Part 2 of the form as follows:

1. Request the nonimmigrant classification "TN-2" for a Mexican citizen beneficiary.

2. For new employment, check box a.

3. Since this is for new employment, put "N/A" on the line.

4. Since the professional must obtain a visa from a U.S. consulate, the employer should check box a of the Requested Action section.

5. The petition can be used for only one TN professional. The employer should indicate "one" in the space provided.

Part 3 of the form is for information about the employee. The employer should put "N/A" in the first part, since the petition will not be for an entertainment group. The professional employee's name, date of birth, country of birth, and social security number, or "none" must be entered. An "A number" is an alien number. These are issued to individuals who have applied for and been granted permanent residence, who have applied for asylum, or who are in deportation proceedings. Most TN nonimmigrants will not have an A number, and if that is the case the employer will enter "N/A" in the space provided. If the professional is in the United States, in another status such as an H-1B, the employer must include the date of the employee's original arrival in the United States, the number on the employee's current I-94, the current status from the I-94, and the date that the I-94, and therefore the status, expires.

Part 4 of the INS form I-129 provides information regarding other INS applications and procedures. The employer must include in section a a consulate address in a foreign country (in this case, Mexico) that the employee will visit to obtain the visa. The employee's foreign address must also be included. In section b the employer must indicate if the employee has a valid passport; this is a requirement. Section c will be answered "yes" if the employer is filing petitions for other employees, and the number of such petitions must be provided in the space provided. This question does not refer to petitions that may have been filed previously, but only ones that accompany the petition in question. Section d is answered "yes" if the employee has lost his or her I-94 for a current, different status. Section e will be answered "yes" if petitions are filed for TD status for family members of the employee who will also be coming to the United States; the number of such other petitions must be noted in the space provided. In section f, indicate if the professional employee is in exclusion or deportation proceedings. If the employer has filed a petition for permanent residence for the professional employee, the answer to section g will be "yes," and an explanation must be given on a paper attached to the petition. If this is the case there will be a problem with approval since TN status requires that there not be any immigrant intent. That means that if the professional wants to become a permanent resident of the United States, he or she cannot have the required nonimmigrant intent of returning home after the TN job is finished. If anyone else has filed a petition for permanent residence for the professional, the answer will be "no." Since this is for new employment in Part 2, answer both questions, and include an explanation if either required a "yes" answer. Section i does not apply since it is not for an entertainment group; because there is no space to indicate "N/A," the employer should not mark any box.

Part 5 of the petition requires information about the employment and employer. The employer must include the job title, a nontechnical description of the job, the address where the person will work (which can be "the same as in Part 1"), an indication if the job is a full-time or part-time position, the wages, and other compensation, including how it is earned and the amount. The dates of the intended employment should include a month, day, and year. The employer should ensure that the start date will allow time to process the application and obtain the visa at a consulate. The employer must include a brief description of the type of business (for example, bank, manufacturer of electronic equipment, or research facility), the current number of employees in the organization named in part 1 of the petition, and the gross and net annual income of the employer.

The petition must be signed in Part 6 by a person authorized to sign such documents in the company. The person must print or type his or her name and date the petition. If an attorney represents the employer and completes the petition, the attorney will complete and sign Part 7. If there is no attorney, the employer should put "N/A" in each box of Part 7.

Submitting the Petition

An employer filing a petition on behalf of a citizen of Mexico seeking classification as a TN professional must file supporting documentation at the same time. This supporting documentation must include

1. A labor condition from the Secretary of Labor.
2. Evidence that the beneficiary meets the minimum education requirements or alternative credentials requirements of NAFTA. This documentation may consist

of licenses, degrees, diplomas, certificates, or evidence of membership in professional organizations. Degrees, diplomas, or certificates received by the beneficiary from educational institutions not located within Mexico, Canada, or the United States must be accompanied by an evaluation by a reliable credentials evaluation service that specializes in evaluating foreign educational credentials. Evidence of experience should consist of letters from former employers, or if formerly self-employed, business records attesting to such self-employment. All documents must have an English translation certified by the translator to be accurate.

3. A statement from the prospective employer in the United States specifically stating the profession in which the beneficiary will be engaging and containing a full description of the nature of the duties that the beneficiary will be performing. The statement must set forth licensure requirements for the state or locality of intended employment, or if no license is required, the non-existence of such requirements for the professional activity to be engaged in.

4. The required fee.

Approval and Validity of Petition

The INS will notify the employer-petitioner of the approval of the petition on form I-797, "Notice of Action." The approval notice will include the beneficiary's name, classification, NAFTA profession, and the petition's period of validity with a starting and end date. If the petition is approved before the date the petitioner indicated that employment will begin, the approved petition and approval notice will show the actual dates requested by the petitioner as the validity period, not to exceed one year. If the petition is approved after the date the petitioner indicated employment will begin, the approved petition and approval notice will show a validity period commencing with the date of approval and ending with the date requested by the petitioner, as long as that date does not exceed one year. If the period of employment requested by the petitioner exceeds one year, the petition will be approved for only one year.

Denial of Petition

When an adverse decision is proposed on the basis of derogatory information of which the petitioner is unaware, the INS will notify the petitioner of the intent to deny the petition and the basis for the denial. The petitioner may inspect and rebut the evidence and will be granted a period of thirty days in which to do so. All relevant rebuttal material will be considered in making a final decision. The petitioner will be notified of the decision, the reasons for the denial, and the right to appeal the denial.

Revocation of Approval of Petition

The employer-petitioner must immediately notify the INS of any changes in the terms and conditions of employment of a Mexican citizen professional that may affect eligibility under the INA. An amended petition should be filed when the petitioner continues to employ the beneficiary. If the petitioner no longer employs the beneficiary, the petitioner must send a letter explaining the change(s) to the director who approved the petition.

The director may revoke a petition at any time, even after the validity of the petition has expired. The approval of an unexpired petition is automatically revoked if the petitioner goes out of business, files a written withdrawal of the petition, or notifies the INS that the beneficiary is no longer employed by the petitioner.

Revocation on Notice

The INS will send to the petitioner a notice of intent to revoke the petition in relevant part if it finds that

1. The beneficiary is no longer employed by the petitioner in the capacity specified in the petition;
2. The statement of facts contained in the petition was not true and correct;
3. The petitioner violated the terms or conditions of the approved petition;
4. The petitioner violated requirements of the act; or
5. The approval of the petition violated the regulations or involved gross error.

The notice of intent to revoke will contain a detailed statement of the grounds for the revocation and the time period allowed for the petitioner's rebuttal. The petitioner may submit evidence in rebuttal within thirty days of the date of the notice. The INS will consider all relevant evidence presented in deciding whether to revoke the petition.

Appeal of a Denial or Revocation of a Petition

A denied petition may be appealed. A petition that has been revoked on notice may be appealed. Automatic revocations may not be appealed.

Consular Processing

The Mexican citizen beneficiary of an approved form I-129 granting classification as a TN professional will be admitted to the U.S. for the validity period of the approved petition upon presentation of a valid TN visa issued by a U.S. consular officer and a copy of the U.S. employer's statement.

However, the approval of a petition by the INS does not establish that the Mexican citizen professional is eligible to receive a nonimmigrant TN visa.[4] The professional will have to demonstrate to the consular officer that he or she meets all of the qualifications required for temporary entry in TN status. The professional should take all documentation related to the job, his or her professional credentials, and the address of his or her permanent residence in Mexico when meeting with the consular officer. Upon approval, the Mexican citizen will be provided a visa and form I-94 bearing the legend "multiple entry."

NOTES

1. 8 CFR § 214.6(e).
2. See INA § 214(e)(5), § 212(m), and § 212(n); and 8 CFR § 214.2(h).
3. 8 CFR § 214.6(d).
4. 22 CFR § 41.59(4)(b).

Chapter 7

Extension of Stay

Trade NAFTA (TN) professionals can be granted an extension of stay for a period of up to one year. Even though the purpose of TN status is to allow temporary entry to the United States, there is no limit on the number of times a TN professional can be granted an extension of stay. Once in the United States in TN status, a professional can stay in the United States in his or her job virtually forever by applying for extensions.

As in most aspects of obtaining TN status, the procedure is different for citizens of Canada and Mexico.

CANADIAN CITIZEN TN EXTENSIONS

Canadian citizen TNs can obtain an extension of stay by one of two procedures. They can stay in the United States and file a petition with the Northern Service Center, or they can leave the country and reenter at the border. Which method is preferred will depend on whether the professional has the time or desire to leave the United States, how much time exists before the current TN status expires, if the curent status has expired, and whether the professional wants to take advantage of a lesser fee.

Filing at the Service Center

If the current TN status has not yet expired, the employer-petitioner may file the petition at the INS Northern Service Center (now renamed the Nebraska Service Center) to extend the TN status of a Canadian professional employee. The employee must be physically present in the United States at the time the employer files the petition for the extension of stay.

Completing the Petition

The extension is requested on INS form I-129. It is important that every part of the form be completed; information may be typed or printed in black ink. If a question or information box does not apply to the employer or the employee, the employer should indicate this by putting "N/A" in the space provided.

The petition should be filed no more than four months before the date that the extension will start but at least 45 days before the expiration of the employee's current TN status. The INS takes about 45 days to approve an extension of a TN status. If the petition is filed too late, the employee's current status may expire. The employee may then be required to cease working and leave the United States until his or her new status is approved. Generally if the petition is filed before the current status has expired, the INS will approve the extension of stay without requiring the employee to leave and reenter.

Part 1 of the form requires the employer's name, address, and IRS Tax Identification Number. The employer will complete Part 2 of the form as follows:

1. Request the nonimmigrant classification of "TN-1," which indicates that the beneficiary is a citizen of Canada for INS statistical purposes.

2. For an extension of employment without any change in employer, check box b.

3. If the petition is for an extension of employment, there may have been a previous petition for the current TN status. If the petition is for a first extension after the professional obtained his or her original TN status by making an application at a port of entry, there will be no prior petition number and the employer should enter "N/A" on the line. If this is a second or subsequent petition to extend TN status for the same employer, the employer should enter the Receipt Number from the INS form I-797 that was issued to extend the status on the last petition. The Receipt Number is found in the top left corner of form I-797.

4. Since the petition is to extend the status of a professional who is in the United States, the employer should check box c of the Requested Action section.

5. The petition can be used to apply for the extension of only one TN professional. The employer should indicate "one" in the space provided.

Part 3 of the form is for information about the employee. The employer should put "N/A" in the first part, since the petition is not for an entertainment group. The professional employee's name, date of birth, country of birth, and social security number must be included. An "A number" is an alien number. These are issued to individuals who have applied for and been granted permanent residence, who have applied for asylum, or who are in deportation proceedings. Most TN nonimmigrants will not have an A number, and if that is the case the employer will enter "N/A" in the space provided. If the professional is in the United States, the employer must include the date of the employee's original arrival in the United States, the number on the employee's current I-94, the current status from the I-94 (TN), and the date that the I-94, and therefore the status, expires.

Part 4 of the INS form I-129 provides information regarding other INS applications and procedures. The employer must include in section a a consulate, pre-flight inspection, or port of entry address in a foreign country (in this case, Canada), in case the employee will be out of the United States when approval for the extension is granted. The employee's foreign address must also be included. In section b the employer must indicate if the employee has a valid passport, and for Canadian citizens the choice can be "not required to have a passport," although it is recommended that Canadians have a valid passport. Section c will be answered "yes" if the employer is filing petitions for other employees, and the number of such petitions must be provided in the space provided. This question does not refer to petitions that may have been filed previously, but only to those that accompany the petition in question. In section d a replacement I-94 will be needed if the employee has lost the current one. Section e will be answered "yes" if petitions are filed to extend the TD status of family members of the employee; the number of such other petitions must be noted in the space provided. In section f indicate if the professional employee is in exclusion or deportation proceedings. If the employer has filed a petition for permanent residence for the professional employee, the answer to section g will be "yes," and an explanation must be given on a paper attached to the petition. This can present a problem and a denial of the extension since an alien in TN status may not have the dual intent of being both a nonimmigrant in TN status and an immigrant who wants to reside in the United States permanently. If anyone else has filed a petition for permanent residence for the professional, the answer will be "no." Section h does not apply because this petition is being used for an extension of stay and not for a new employee and the choice should be "no." Section i does not apply since the petition is not for an entertainment group; the employer should not mark any box because there is no space to indicate "N/A."

Part 5 of the petition requires information about the employment and employer. The employer must include the job title, a nontechnical description of the job, the address where the person will work (which can be "the same as in Part 1"), an indication if the job is a full-time or part-time position, the wages, and other compensation, including how it is earned and the amount. The dates of the intended employment should include a month, day, and year. The employer should ensure that the start date is no more than the next day after the expiration of the current TN status. If there is a gap of even one day, the employee will be out of status and will have to leave the United States to avoid being subject to potential penalties for being out of status. The employer must include a brief description of the type of business (for example, bank, manufacturer of electronic equipment, or research facility), the current number of employees in the organization named in part 1 of the petition, and the gross and net annual income of the employer.

The petition must be signed in Part 6 by a person authorized to sign such documents in the company. The person must print or type his or her name and date the petition. If an attorney represents the employer and completes the petition, the attorney will complete and sign Part 7. If there is no attorney, the employer should put "N/A" in each box of Part 7.

Submitting the Petition

The petition must be accompanied by

1. The prescribed fee. The INS will accept a corporate check, certified check, or money order.
2. A statement of the job position to be held by the beneficiary, including the name of the profession, a full description of the nature of the duties the professional will be performing, the anticipated length of stay, and the arrangements for remuneration. This statement must be included even though it repeats information provided on the INS form I-129.
3. Evidence that the beneficiary meets the educational or other requirements for the profession. A photocopy of degrees, resumes listing experience, and other documents are sufficient. Petitioners should not send originals, since these will not be returned by INS. Any document not in English must have attached a translation into English certified and signed by the translator. This may also be a photocopy. The petitioner, or the beneficiary, must have the original documents available if requested by the INS.
4. Evidence of Canadian citizenship. This can be a photocopy of the birth certificate, passport, or naturalization document issued by the Canadian authorities. If it is not in English, it will require an English translation.
5. Evidence that all licensure requirements, if any, have been met. If the job is one that sometimes requires, or appears to require, a license, and does not for the beneficiary's employment, the petitioner should include a letter explaining why no license is required. This may apply to lawyers who are working in-house and are not required to join the state bar; to teachers who are providing special classes and are not part of the public school system; for medical professionals who are not practicing their specialty but are teaching or providing other services; and similar professions.

The employer should mail the petition, all supporting documents, and the filing fee with a cover letter to the Northern Service Center by certified mail. Employers should keep a photocopy of the complete petition and all supporting documents and attach the receipt for the certified mail when it is received. Although this is rare, petitions and documents have been lost in INS service centers, which receive tens of thousands of packages each week. About two to three weeks after receiving the package, the INS will mail a Receipt Notice on INS form I-797 to the employer. This will state that the INS has received the petition package and fee and will indicate how long it will take to make a decision on the petition. It will also include a telephone number that can be called to get an automated update on the status of the petition.

Once the petition is filed, the employee has an automatic 240-day extension of the work authorization until the extension is granted. This only applies, however, if the petition is filed in a timely manner before the current TN status has expired.

Readmission at the Border

Canadian professionals with TN status have the option to extend their status by making an application at a port of entry. In this case the employer must write a new letter addressed to the INS that states that the employer desires to continue to employ the named person as a professional in a named category of professions listed in NAFTA, with certain job duties related to the profession; that the employee meets the education and experience requirements for the profession; that any licensing requirements have been met by the employee or are not required. The employer must also specify the method and amount of remuneration.

The professional employee must take this letter; proof of education and experience (degrees, resumes, and letters from former employers); proof of Canadian citizenship (in the form of a birth certificate, passport, or naturalization certificate); English translations for any documents not in English; and the appropriate fee to a port of entry. The application for extension of TN status is made in a manner similar to the original application for TN status and will be approved or disapproved on the spot.

This is a good choice of procedures for Canadian citizens who (1) live close to the Canadian border, (2) have little time before the expiration of their current TN status, (3) will be going out of the United States shortly before the expiration of their current status and will be reentering at a port of entry to continue their job, or (4) want to save money by paying the lower fee at a port of entry than that required to be submitted with a petition.

MEXICAN CITIZEN TN EXTENSIONS

For Mexican citizen professionals, there is only one method to extend the stay of the employee. The employer must file a petition to extend the TN status of a Mexican citizen professional employee. The employer must also request a petition extension at the same time by filing either a new

Labor Condition Application or a photocopy of the prior certification on form ETA 9027 for a registered nurse, or form ETA 9035 for all other professionals. The employer will continue to have this form on file with the Federal Department of Labor for the period of employment of the Mexican citizen. The employee must be physically present in the United States at the time the employer files the petition for the extension of stay.

The petition should be filed no more than four months before the date that the extension will start but at least 45 days before the expiration of the employee's current TN status. The INS takes about 45 days to approve an extension of a TN status. Even though there is an automatic 240-day extension of work authorization when a petition for a extension of TN status is filed in a timely manner, it is usually the best practice to file as soon as possible to ensure the employee has valid documentation in case he or she needs to travel out of the country and so the professional's family members have valid extensions of their TD status.

Completing the Petition

The extension is requested on INS form I-129 and sent to the INS Northern Service Center. It is important that every part of the form be completed; information can be typed or printed in black ink. If a question or information box does not apply to the employer or the employee, the employer should indicate this by putting "N/A" in the space provided.

Part 1 of the form requires the employer's name, address, and IRS Tax Identification Number. The employer will complete Part 2 of the form as follows:

1. Request the nonimmigrant classification of "TN-2" which indicates that the beneficiary is a citizen of Mexico for INS statistical purposes.
2. For an extension of employment without any change in employer, check box b.
3. If the petition is for an extension of employment, there may have been a previous petition for the current TN status. If the petition is for a first extension after the professional obtained his or her original TN status by making an application at a port of entry, there will be no prior petition number, and the employer should enter "N/A" on the line. If this is a second or subsequent petition to extend TN status for the same employee, the employer should enter the Receipt Number from the INS form I-797 that was issued to extend the status on the last petition. The Receipt Number is found in the top left corner of the form I-797.
4. Since the petition is to extend the status of a professional who is in the United States, the employer should check box c of the Requested Action section.
5. The petition can be used to apply for the extension of only one TN professional. The employer should indicate "N/A" in the space provided.

Part 4 of the INS form I-129 provides information regarding other INS applications and procedures. The employer must include in section a a

consulate, pre-flight inspection, or port of entry address in a foreign country
(in this case, Mexico), in case the employee will be out of the United States
when approval for the extension is granted. The employee's foreign address
must also be included. In section b the employer must indicate if the employee has a valid passport. Section c will be answered "yes" if the employer is filing petitions for other employees, and the number of such
petitions must be provided in the space provided. This question does not
refer to petitions that may have been filed previously, but only ones that
accompany the petition in question. In section d a replacement I-94 will be
needed if the employee has lost the current one. Section e will be answered
"yes" if petitions are filed to extend the TD status of family members of
the employee, and the number of such other petitions must be noted in the
space provided. In section f indicate if the professional employee is in exclusion or deportation proceedings. If the employer has filed a petition for
permanent residence for the professional employee, the answer to section
g will be "yes," and an explanation must be given on a paper attached to
the petition. This can present a problem and a denial of the extension since
an alien in TN status may not have the dual intent of being both a nonimmigrant in TN status and an immigrant who wants to reside in the
United States permanently. If anyone else has filed a petition for permanent
residence for the professional, the answer will be "no." Section h does not
apply because this petition is being used for an extension of stay and not
for a new employee, and the choice should be "no." Section i does not
apply since the petition is not for an entertainment group. The employer
should not mark any box because there is no space to indicate "N/A."

Part 5 of the petition requires information about the employment and
employer. The employer must include the job title, a nontechnical description of the job (including whether it is full time or part time); the address
where the person will work (which can be "the same as in Part 1"); and
the wages and other compensation (including how they are earned and the
amounts). The dates of the intended employment should include a month,
day, and year. The employer should ensure that the start date is no more
than the next day after the expiration of the current TN status. If there is
a gap of even one day, the employee will be out of status and will have to
leave the United States to avoid being subject to potential penalties for
being out of status. The employer must include a brief description of the
type of business (for example, bank, manufacturer of electronic equipment,
or research facility), the current number of employees for the organization
named in Part 1 of the petition, and the gross and net annual income of
the employer.

The petition must be signed in Part 6 by a person authorized to sign
such documents in the company. The person must print or type his or her
name and date the petition. If an attorney represents the employer and

completes the petition, the attorney will complete and sign Part 7. If there is no attorney, the employer should put "N/A" in each box of Part 7.

Submitting the Petition

The petition must be accompanied by

1. The prescribed fee. The INS will accept a corporate check, certified check, or money order.

2. A statement of the job position to be held by the beneficiary, including the name of the profession, a full description of the nature of the duties the professional will be performing, the anticipated length of stay, and the arrangements for remuneration. This statement must be included even though it repeats information provided on the INS form I-129.

3. Evidence that the beneficiary meets the educational or other requirements for the profession. A photocopy of degrees, resumes listing experience, and other documents are sufficient. Do not send originals, they will not be returned. Any document not in English must have attached a translation into English certified and signed by the translator. This may also be a photocopy. The petitioner or the beneficiary must have the original documents available if requested by the INS.

4. Evidence of Mexican citizenship. This can be a photocopy of the birth certificate, passport, or naturalization document issued by the Mexican authorities. If it is not in English, it will require an English translation.

5. Evidence that all licensure requirements, if any, have been met. If the job is one that sometimes requires, or appears to require, a license, and does not for the beneficiary's employment, include a letter explaining why no license is required. This may apply for such professionals as lawyers who are working in-house and are not required to join the state bar, teachers who are providing special classes and are not part of the public school system, and medical professionals who are not practicing their specialty but are teaching or providing other services.

6. A new ETA 9029 for a registered nurse, or ETA 9035 for all other professionals, or a copy of one previously on file with the federal Department of Labor that is still valid, and a request for extension.

The employer should mail the petition, all supporting documents, and the filing fee with a cover letter to the Northern Service Center by certified mail. Employers should keep a photocopy of the complete petition and all supporting documents and attach the receipt for the certified mail when it is received. Although this is rare, petitions and documents have been lost in INS service centers, which receive tens of thousands of packages each week. About two to three weeks after receiving the package, the INS will mail a Receipt Notice on INS form I-797 to the employer. This will state that the INS has received the petition package and fee and will indicate how long it will take to make a decision on the petition. It will also include a telephone number that can be called to get an automated update on the status of the petition.

Chapter 8

Changing or Adding Employers

When searching for a professional to fill a job opening, a company may find the person it wants to hire is someone who is already working in the United States with TN status. The company may hire such a person either as a part-time employee who takes the job as a second job while continuing with the first job, or as a full-time employee who will resign from his or her present job. A company should consider five factors when making the decision to hire someone who is already in TN status:

1. the length of time required for the TN professional to obtain INS approval for accepting the new employment,

2. the documentary support required to assist the employee to obtain an adjusted TN status,

3. the cost involved in obtaining adjusted TN status,

4. the effect of a time gap between the jobs for the TN professional who leaves one job to start another, and

5. any coordination required between the two employers.

The length of time required for the TN professional to obtain INS approval will affect the effective start date of the employment. The time period will be over 45 days for a Mexican citizen professional, up to 45 days for a Canadian citizen professional who files at the service center, and as short as one day for a Canadian citizen professional who seeks readmission at a border. The necessity for this time period may influence a company's decision to hire someone who needs 45 days or more to become legally eligible to start work.

The minimum documentary support required will be a letter offering employment and stipulating the details required to support a TN application for a Canadian citizen professional. The maximum documentary support will be when the company provides all documents for a Mexican citizen professional. The amount of documentary support a company will offer will depend on its expertise in providing this documentation, the availability of staff to provide the documentation, the time period they have to complete the documentation, and the expectations of the new employee for support and legal assistance as part of a hiring bonus.

The cost of obtaining an adjusted TN status for a new employee who has an existing TN status can include the time required of present employees to complete the required documentation, INS filing fees, fax and delivery charges, and travel to a border to make an application. Depending on what is negotiated between the employer and the new employee, these costs may be all paid by the employer, or shared between the employer and the new employee.

If a TN professional leaves one job to start work with another employer, there may be a time between when he or she leaves the prior job and when he or she can obtain an adjusted TN status that will permit employment at the subsequent job. If this is the case, there can be a problem for the professional, who will be out of status for a period of time. The day the TN professional ceases employment with the first employer, his or her TN status ends, even though the I-94 indicates a later expiry date, and there are no INS officials knocking on the door telling the professional to leave. Being out of status means being an illegal immigrant, and the professional can be subject to penalties that will restrict future entries and visas. Bridging this time gap is something that must be handled correctly.

If the professional gives notice to the first employer so the last day of work will be the day before the new job starts, and he or she is able to obtain an adjusted TN status before the first day of the new job, there is no problem. However, often when a professional employee gives notice, an employer will offer a payment package and ask the employee to leave that day. If that happens to someone in TN status, they will immediately be out of status and be required to leave the United States. There is one way an employee could prevent this from happening, but it is only available to Canadian citizens. The employee must make a quick trip to the border and apply for an adjusted TN status for the new employer. With new status in hand, the employee, who now can no longer be legally employed by the first employer, would give notice that he or she is quitting that day.

Any other method requires the cooperation of the two employers to ensure that the time gap between the jobs is covered during the acquisition of the adjusted TN status. For example, if a professional had a job on a project that ended on November 30, and the employer did not intend to hire the professional for another project, the professional could find another job and file an adjustment application with the service center in early October stating that the new TN status would commence on December 1. In this case there would be no time gap during which the professional would be out of status. This example would work for a Canadian professional; for a Mexican professional, an additional time period would be needed to obtain a new filing of a Labor Condition Application with the Secretary of Labor. The problem with this scenario is that the professional may not find a new employer that is willing to wait for two months for the employee to start work.

Another way to achieve the result with cooperation between employers is for the employee to obtain an adjustment of status by the addition of an employer so the I-94 would include both employers. This would be a temporary solution that would require two adjustments. The first would be to request the addition of the second employer. Once this was granted, the employee could start to work for the second employer and still work for the first one. Once the first job ended, and the employee only worked for the second employer, a second adjustment would be required to remove the first employer. This would double the time and cost of making applications, which for a Canadian citizen living close to the border would be a slight inconvenience, but for a Mexican citizen would be more costly and lengthy.

If the TN professional has family members in the United States in TD status, each family member will have to make a renewal of his or her status to coincide with each change for the TN professional, since their status is derived from that of the professional and ends when it does. This could be very costly, time consuming, and inconvenient for the family.

PROCEDURE FOR CANADIAN CITIZENS

Canadian citizen professionals can choose between two methods to change or add an employer during their period of admission. They can file at the service center or seek readmission at a port of entry.

Port of Entry Procedure

The port of entry procedure for replacing or adding a new employer is the same as for the initial application for a Canadian citizen professional seeking TN status. In this case, the new employer must write a new letter addressed to the INS that states that the employer desires to employ the named person (by replacing the former employer or being added as a concurrent employer) as a professional in a named category of professions listed in NAFTA, with certain job duties related to the profession; that the employee meets the education and experience requirements for the profession; and that any licensing requirements have been met by the employee or are not required. The letter should include the name and address of the former or other concurrent employer, details of the job, and the method and amount of remuneration.

The professional employee must take this letter; proof of education and experience (degrees, resumes, and letters from former employers); proof of Canadian citizenship (in the form of a birth certificate, passport, or naturalization certificate); English translations for any documents not in English; and the appropriate fee to a port of entry. The professional should also take a complete copy of the application and approval of the current TN status. The application for change or addition of a new employer for TN status is made in a manner similar to the original application for TN status and will be approved or disapproved on the spot.

This is a good choice of procedures for anyone who (1) lives close to the Canadian border, (2) has little time before the new job is to start, (3) will be going out of the United States for a trip and will be reentering at a port of entry, or (4) wants to save money by paying the lower fee at a port of entry than that required to be submitted with a petition.

Filing at the Service Center

The new employer, not the professional, must file an INS form I-129, supporting documents, and the required fee at the Northern Service Center. The supporting documents that are required include

1. A letter from the new employer describing the services to be performed, the time needed to render such services, and the terms of remuneration for the services.
2. Evidence that the beneficiary meets the educational or other requirements for the profession. A photocopy of degrees, resumes listing experience, and other documents are sufficient.
3. Evidence of Canadian citizenship. This can be a photocopy of the birth certificate, passport, or naturalization document issued by the Canadian authorities. If the evidence is not in English, it will require an English translation.
4. Evidence that all licensure requirements, if any, have been met. If the job is one that sometimes requires, or appears to require, a license, and does not for the beneficiary's employment, a letter explaining why no license is required should be included.
5. The prescribed fee.

Completing the Petition

If at all possible, an employer should obtain a copy of the filed application, all supporting documentation submitted, letters of employment offers, approval notices, and all correspondence with the INS from the previous employer. The information on these documents will be required to complete the petition.

It is important that every part of the form be completed; information can be typed or printed in black ink. If a question or information box does not apply to the employer or the employee, the employer should indicate this by putting "N/A" in the space provided.

To allow the service center time to process the petition, it should be filed at least 45 days before the new employment is to begin. The employee will not be able to start the new job until an approval notice is received from the INS naming the new employer who will replace, or be in addition to, the former employer.

Part 1 of the form requires the new employer's name, address, and IRS Tax Identification Number. The employer will complete Part 2 of the form as follows:

1. Request the nonimmigrant classification of "TN-1," which indicates that the beneficiary is a citizen of Canada for INS statistical purposes or "TN-2" for a Mexican citizen beneficiary.

2. For a change in employer, check box c. For a new concurrent employer, check box d.

3. The employer should enter the Receipt Number from the INS form I-797 that was issued to the former (or other concurrent) employer. The Receipt Number is found in the top left corner of the form I-797.

4. Since the petition is to replace or add an employer of a professional who is in the United States, the employer should check box c of the Requested Action section.

5. The petition can be used to apply for the extension of only one TN professional. The employer should indicate "one" in the space provided.

Part 3 of the form is for information about the employee. The employer should put "N/A" in the first part since the petition is not for an entertainment group. The professional employee's name, date of birth, country of birth, and social security number must be included. An "A number" is an alien number. It is issued to individuals who have applied for and been granted permanent residence, who have applied for asylum, or who are in deportation proceedings. Most TN nonimmigrants will not have an A number; if that is the case, the employer will enter "N/A" in the space provided. If the professional employee has been approved for permanent residence under another petition and grounds, an A number will have been issued, and it must be included here. If the professional is in the United States, the employer must include the date of the employee's original arrival in the United States, the number on the employee's current I-94, the current status from the I-94 (TN), and the date that the I-94, and therefore the status, expires.

Part 4 of the INS form I-129 provides information regarding other INS applications and procedures. The employer must include in section a a consulate, pre-flight inspection, or port of entry address in a foreign country, (which will likely be in Canada), in case the employee will be out of the United States when approval for the extension is granted. The employee's foreign address must also be included. In section b, the employer must indicate if the employee has a valid passport, and for Canadian citizens the choice can be "not required to have a passport," although it is recommended that Canadians have a valid passport. Section c will be answered "yes" if the employer is filing petitions for other employees, and the number of such petitions must be provided in the space provided. This question does not refer to petitions that may have been filed previously, but only ones that accompany the petition in question. Section d should be answered "yes" if the employee has lost his or her I-94. Section e should be answered "yes" if petitions are filed to extend the TD status of family members of the employee, and the number of such other petitions must be noted in the space provided. This will be required if there is a change in employers, and if the concurrent employer's job will last longer than the first employer's job. In section f, indicate if the professional employee is in exclusion or deportation proceedings. If the employer has filed a petition for permanent residence for the professional employee, the answer to section g will be "yes," and an explanation must be given on a statement attached to the petition. If this is the case, there may be a problem with approval since TN status requires that there not be any immigrant intent. That means that if the professional wants to become a permanent resident of the United States, he or she cannot have the required nonimmigrant intent of returning home after the TN job is finished. If anyone else has filed a petition for permanent residence for the professional, the answer will be "no." Section h is no, since this is not for new employment in Part 2. Section i does not apply since the petition is not for an entertainment group. The employer should not mark any box because there is no space to indicate "N/A."

Part 5 of the petition requires information about the employment and employer. The employer must include the job title; a nontechnical description of the job (including whether it is full time or part time); the address where the person will work (which can be "the same as in Part 1"); and the wages and other compensation (including how they are earned and the amounts.) The dates of the intended employment should include a month, day, and year. The employer should ensure that the start date is no later than the next day after the expiration of the current TN status if there is a change in employers. If there is a gap of even one day, the employee will be out of status and will have to leave the United States and obtain a visa at a consulate. The employer must include a brief description of the type of business (for example, bank, manufacturer of electronic equipment, or research facility), the current number of employees in the organization named in Part 1 of the petition, and the gross and net annual income of the employer.

The petition must be signed in Part 6 by a person authorized to sign such documents in the company. The person must print or type his or her name and date the petition. If an attorney represents the employer and completes the petition, the attorney will complete and sign Part 7. If there is no attorney, the employer should put "N/A" in each box of Part 7.

Submitting the Petition

The petition must be accompanied by

1. The prescribed fee. INS will accept a corporate check, certified check, or money order.

2. A statement of the job position to be held by the beneficiary, including the name of the profession, a full description of the nature of the duties the professional will be performing, the anticipated length of stay, and the arrangements for remuneration. This statement must be included even though it repeats information provided on the INS form I-129.

3. Evidence that the beneficiary meets the educational or other requirements for the profession. A photocopy of degrees, resumes listing experience, and other documents are sufficient. Do not send originals, they will not be returned. Any document not in English must have attached a translation into English certified and signed by the translator. This may also be a photocopy. The petitioner or the beneficiary must have the original documents available if requested by the INS.

4. Evidence of Canadian citizenship. This can be a photocopy of the birth certificate, passport, or naturalization document issued by the Canadian authorities. If it is not in English, it will require an English translation.

5. Evidence that all licensure requirements, if any, have been met. If the job is one that sometimes requires, or appears to require, a license, and does not for the beneficiary's employment, include a letter explaining why no license is required.

Upon receiving an Approval Notice from the INS, the employee may commence work with the replacement or new concurrent employer.

PROCEDURE FOR MEXICAN CITIZENS

Employers who want to hire a citizen of Mexico in TN status to replace a former employer or to become an additional employer have only one procedure to follow. An INS Form I-129 and supporting documents must be filed at the Northern Service Center.

Filing at the Service Center

The new employer, not the professional, must file an INS form I-129, supporting documents, and the required fee at the Northern Service Center. The supporting documents that are required include

1. A letter from the new employer describing the services to be performed, the time needed to render such services, and the terms of remuneration for the services.
2. Evidence that the beneficiary meets the educational or other requirements for the profession. A photocopy of degrees, resumes listing experience, and other documents are sufficient.
3. Evidence of Mexican citizenship. This can be a photocopy of the birth certificate, passport, or naturalization document issued by the Mexican authorities. If it is not in English it will require an English translation.
4. Evidence that all licensure requirements, if any, have been met. If the job is one that sometimes requires, or appears to require, a license, and does not for the beneficiary's employment, include a letter explaining why no license is required.
5. A new ETA 9029 for a registered nurse, or ETA 9035 for all other professionals, or a copy of one previously on file with the federal Department of Labor that is still valid.
6. The prescribed fee.

Completing the Petition

If at all possible, an employer should obtain a copy of the filed application, all supporting documentation submitted, letters of employment offer, approval notices, and all correspondence with the INS from the previous employer. The information on these documents will be required to complete the petition.

It is important that every part of the form be completed; information can be typed or printed in black ink. If a question or information box does not apply to the employer or the employee, the employer should indicate this by putting "N/A" in the space provided.

To allow the service center time to process the petition, it should be filed at least 45 days before the new employment is to begin. The employee will not be able to start the new job until an approval notice is received from INS naming the new employer who will replace, or be in addition to, the former employer.

Part 1 of the form requires the new employer's name, address, and IRS Tax Identification Number. The employer will complete Part 2 of the form as follows:

1. Request the nonimmigrant classification "TN-2" for a Mexican citizen beneficiary.

2. For a change in employer, check box c. For a new concurrent employer, check box d.

3. The employer should enter the Receipt Number from the INS form I-797 that was issued to the former (or other concurrent) employer. The Receipt Number is found in the top left corner of the form I-797.

4. Since the petition is to replace or add an employer of a professional who is in the United States, the employer should check box c of the Requested Action section.

5. The petition can be used to apply for the extension of only one TN professional. The employer should indicate "one" in the space provided.

Part 3 of the form is for information about the employee. The employer should put "N/A" in the first part since the petition will not be for an entertainment group. The professional employee's name, date of birth, country of birth, and social security number must be included. An "A number" is an alien number. These are issued to individuals who have applied for and been granted permanent residence, who have applied for asylum, or who are in deportation proceedings. Most TN nonimmigrants won't have an A number, and if that is the case, the employer will enter "N/A" in the space provided. If the professional employee has been approved for permanent residence under another petition and grounds, an A number will have been issued, and it must be included here. If the professional is in the United States, the employer must include the date of the employee's original arrival in the United States, the number on the employee's current I-94, the current status from the I-94 (TN), and the date that the I-94, and therefore the status, expires.

Part 4 of the INS form I-129 provides information regarding other INS applications and procedures. The employer must include in section a a consulate, pre-flight inspection, or port of entry address in a foreign country, (in this case, Mexico), in case the employee will be out of the United States when approval for the extension is granted. The employee's foreign address must also be included. In section b the employer must indicate if the employee has a valid passport. Section c will be answered "yes" if the employer is filing petitions for other employees, and the number of such petitions must be provided in the space provided. This question does not refer to petitions that may have been filed previously, but only to those that accompany the petition in question. Section d should be answered "yes" if the employee has lost his or her I-94. Section e should be answered "yes" if petitions are filed to extend the TD status of family members of the employee, and the number of such other petitions must be noted in the space provided. This will be required if there is a change in employers and the concurrent employer's job will last longer than the first employer's job. In section f, indicate if the professional employee is in exclusion or deportation proceedings. If the employer has filed a petition for permanent residence for the professional employee, the answer to section g will be "yes," and an explanation must be given on a paper attached to the petition. If this is the case, there may be a problem with approval since TN status requires that there not be any immigrant intent. That means that if the professional wants to become a permanent resident of the United States, he or she cannot have the required nonimmigrant intent of returning home after the TN job is finished. If anyone else has filed a petition for permanent residence for the professional, the answer will be "no." Section h should be answered "no." Section i does not apply since it is not for an entertainment group; the employer should not mark any box because there is no space to indicate "N/A."

Part 5 of the petition requires information about the employment and employer. The employer must include the job title, a nontechnical description of the job (including whether it is full time or part time); the address where the person will work (which can be "the same as in Part 1"); and the wages and other compensation (including how they are earned and the amounts). The dates of the intended employment should include a month, day, and year. The employer should ensure that the start date is no later than the next day after the expiration of the current TN status if there is a change in employers. If there is a gap of even one day, the employee will be out of status and will have to leave the United States and obtain a visa at a consulate. The employer must include a brief description of the type of business (for example, bank, manufacturer of electronic equipment, or research facility), the current number of employees in the organization named in part 1 of the petition, and the gross and net annual income of the employer.

The petition must be signed in Part 6 by a person authorized to sign such documents in the company. The person must print or type his or her name and date the petition. If an attorney represents the employer and completes the petition, the attorney will complete and sign Part 7. If there is no attorney, the employer should put "N/A" in each box of Part 7.

Submitting the Petition

The petition must be accompanied by

1. The prescribed fee. INS will accept a corporate check, certified check, or money order.

2. A statement of the job position to be held by the beneficiary, including the name of the profession, a full description of the duties the professional will be performing, the anticipated length of stay, and the arrangements for remuneration.

This statement must be included even though it repeats information provided on the INS form I-129.

3. Evidence that the beneficiary meets the educational or other requirements for the profession. A photocopy of degrees, resumes listing experience, and other documents are sufficient. Do not send originals, they will not be returned. Any document not in English must have attached a translation into English certified and signed by the translator. This may also be a photocopy. The petitioner or the beneficiary must have the original documents available if requested by the INS.

4. Evidence of Mexican citizenship. This can be a photocopy of the birth certificate, passport, or naturalization document issued by the Mexican authorities. If it is not in English, it will require an English translation.

5. Evidence that all licensure requirements, if any, have been met. If the job is one that sometimes requires, or appears to require, a license, and does not for the beneficiary's employment, include a letter explaining why no license is required.

Upon receiving an Approval Notice from the INS, the employee may commence work with the replacement or new concurrent employer.

Chapter 9

Changing and Ending Employment

There may be times when a TN professional employee must leave the United States before the expiration of his or her status and want to reenter. There may be a substantial change in the job of the TN professional employee. The TN professional employee may be transferred to another job site. The TN professional employee may be terminated from employment. This chapter will discuss each of these situations.

READMISSION AND TEMPORARY EXITS

There are provisions that allow those in TN status to make temporary exits from the United States without adjusting or extending their status.[1]

Canadian Citizens

A Canadian citizen who has TN status may be readmitted to the United States for the remainder of the period authorized on Form I-94 without having to present the letter or supporting documentation that was required to obtain the status, and without paying another fee, provided that the original intended professional activities and employer(s) have not changed. When leaving the United States by air, the passenger's I-94 departure record is generally taken by the airline ticket agent so it can be turned over to the INS. It is likely that most Canadians will leave the United States to return to Canada for a temporary visit by driving a private motor vehicle across the border. Since the I-94 has stamped on it "multiple entry," the TN professional does not have to surrender it to the airline or Canadian border official. The Canadian citizen in TN status can then use this multiple entry I-94 to reenter the United States.

If the Canadian citizen seeking readmission to the United States is no longer in possession of a valid, unexpired form I-94 because it was lost or surrendered when leaving the United States, and the period of initial admission has not lapsed, he or she must present alternate evidence to be readmitted in TN status. This alternate evidence may include, but is not limited to, an INS fee receipt for admission as a TN or a previously issued admission stamp as TN in a passport, and a confirming letter from the U.S. employer(s). A new form I-94 will be issued at the time of readmission bearing the legend "multiple entry."

Mexican Citizens

A Mexican citizen with TN status may be readmitted for the remainder of the period of time authorized on form I-94 provided that the original intended professional activities and employer(s) have not changed. If the Mexican citizen seeking readmission to the United States is no longer in possession of a valid, unexpired form I-94, he or she may be readmitted upon presentation of a valid TN visa and evidence of a previous admission. A new form I-94 will be issued at the time of readmission bearing the legend "multiple entry."

SUBSTANTIAL CHANGE IN JOB

If there is a substantial change in job, the TN professional employee may not remain entitled to the TN status. This is not a matter that is specifically included in the regulations, and is a matter of speculation. For example, if a professional who performed a job requiring specialized knowledge in the sciences was promoted to an administrative position, he or she might not be performing the job duties of a scientist. It could be argued that in this case education or experience in management would be more appropriate for the job.

There is a requirement that any employer must immediately notify the INS of any changes in the terms and conditions of employment that may affect eligibility. This would be required when the employer determined that the employee was moved to a job that was not in the profession and did not require the professional degree or other qualifications, set out by NAFTA. In this case, the INS would revoke the TN status, and the employee would be required to leave the United States or obtain a different nonimmigrant visa status that met the requirements of the job.

TRANSFER OF A PROFESSIONAL

If a Canadian citizen TN professional is transferred to another location by the U.S. employer, and the professional will be performing the same services, the employer does not need to file an amended or replacement Form I-129. This applies only if the transfer is to a branch or another office of the employer. However, if the transfer is to a separately incorporated subsidiary or affiliate, a new petition must be filed to add or change employers. Alternatively, a Canadian citizen may apply for readmission at a port of entry to add or change employers.

If a Mexican citizen TN professional is transferred to an office in another city or state, the employer must obtain a new prevailing wage and Labor Condition Application and file them with the form I-129 at the Northern Service Center before the transfer. The employer must pay the prevailing wage for the new location if the prevailing wage is higher than the present salary. A new prevailing wage and LCA must be obtained even if the move is to a branch of the same employer.

TERMINATING EMPLOYMENT

If the TN professional is no longer employed by the petitioner, either because he or she resigned or was terminated, it is grounds for revocation of the petition. The employer should send notice of the termination of employment to the INS Northern Service Center, and if applicable, to the port of entry at which a Canadian citizen obtained TN status.

NOTE

1. 8 C.F.R. § 214.6(h).

Chapter 10

Professional's Spouse and Unmarried Minor Children

It is likely that the professional a company hires will have a family who will want to move with the TN professional employee. The company can assist new employees to bring their family with them when they move to start their new job. Like most aspects of hiring professionals under NAFTA, the procedure differs depending on whether the professional is a citizen of Canada or Mexico. This chapter will set out the legal elements that are common for citizens of both countries, the specific legal details for Canadian citizens and Mexican citizens, and the strategies and procedures that a company can follow to help family members move to the United States with the TN professional employee.

COMMON ELEMENTS

There are a number of elements that are common for the family members of both Canadian and Mexican TN professionals. The common elements include status, definition of family, the citizenship of the TD family members, and the methods for changing or extending their status. A company can set up a procedure that will apply to all family members of its TN employees.

Status

Family members of a TN professional may obtain the immigration status of "TD," which stands for Trade Dependent. TD is a derivative, temporary status and is based solely on the relationship between the family member and the TN professional spouse or parent. When TN professionals end their employment, their status immediately ends, and so does that of all their TD dependents. Likewise, if the family relationship or qualification ends, so does the TD status of that person.

TD status allows a person to live in the United States for the period of time set out on their immigration documents (I-94, passport, or visa). This period may not exceed one year but can be renewed indefinitely for one-year periods. In addition to being able to live in the United States, a person with TD status may attend school but is not authorized to accept any kind of employment. The children of a TN professional may not take after-school jobs at fast-food restaurants or get a paper route to supplement their allowance, for example. Of course, any family member who meets the re-quirements of another category of nonimmigrant visa that permits work authorization may apply for and be granted such a visa. If they do this, they will no longer have TD status but will have their new nonimmigrant status.

TD status allows the person to leave and reenter the United States as often as they desire, and the TD person's I-94 will be stamped "multiple entry" to allow this. There is no INS fee for the initial application for TD status; however, some ports of entry charge a $6 fee for processing the I-94.

If a TD family member needs a social security number for banking or other purposes, they may apply for one; however, it will be issued with wording on the face of it that it is not for employment. TD family members are entitled to get state driver's licenses and public library cards, and to do all the transactions and activities of other residents, except work.

Definition of Family

Family members that may be granted status include the spouse and children of the TN professional. While it is generally unlawful to ask potential employees if they are married or if they have children, if a company is hiring a NAFTA professional it needs to know this information. The way to avoid any concerns about unlawful hiring practices is to ask for this information after the professional has been verbally hired or given an employment contract. A company needs information about the employee's family to add family members to health and other benefits and so it can provide forms, documentation, or other assistance to help family members obtain their immigration status and move with the employee.

Spouse means a lawful spouse, and "common law" spouses are unlikely to be able to obtain TD status because they will not be able to provide a valid marriage certificate to show the spousal relationship. They will be required to produce a marriage certificate to prove their marriage. If a marriage certificate is in a language other than English, it must have an English translation signed by the translator certifying that it is an exact translation. The term spouse does not include a spouse from a marriage where either spouse was not at the marriage ceremony, unless the marriage is later consummated.[1] An employer may not know the specifics of the marriage ceremony, but this requirement could affect anyone who, for whatever reason, marries someone who is overseas and then attempts to bring them to the United States and obtain immigrant status for them based on this marriage.

The TD status for a spouse will last only as long as the person is the spouse of a TD professional. If the parties divorce, the spouse will no longer be entitled to the TD status. An employer may become aware that a TN professional employee becomes divorced when the employee gives notice to change beneficiaries for a health insurance plan or other benefit provided by the company. In this instance a company should advise the employee that the divorced spouse is no longer entitled to the TD status. This divorced spouse should, immediately upon the divorce becoming final, leave the United States or do whatever is necessary to obtain a new valid immigration status.

A divorce does not affect the TD status of the divorced parties' children. If the custodial parent of TD children is not the TN professional, that custodial parent cannot obtain a derivative immigration status from the children and must return to their home country. The children, however, retain their TD status even when they move to their home country because TN status does not require that they live in the United States; it only allows them to enter and live in the United States. For children whose custodial parent lives in Mexico, or for those living in Canada who are not Canadian citizens, retaining the TD status will allow them to freely visit the non-custodial professional living in the United States with TN status. For Canadian citizen children, retaining TD status is of little advantage because Canadians can freely enter the United States for visits.

There are no provisions for a fiancee to accompany a TN professional. Employees in this situation have two choices. If employees want their fiancee to accompany them, the fiancee can apply for a B-1/B-2 visitor visa. This is easy for Canadian citizens, who are allowed to enter the United States without a passport by just driving to a port of entry or applying at the U.S. customs office at an airport. Mexican citizens who have a border crossing card may enter the United States, but most will be required to obtain a B-1/B-2 visa at a U.S. Consulate in Mexico.

Children of a TN professional may obtain TD status. The Immigration and Nationality Act, 1995 defines child in s. 101(b) as follows:

(1) The term "child" means an unmarried person under twenty-one years of age who is—

(A) a child born in wedlock;

(B) a stepchild, whether or not born out of wedlock, provided the child had not reached the age of eighteen years at the time the marriage creating the status of stepchild occurred;

(C) a child legitimated under the law of the child's residence or domicile, or under the law of the father's residence or domicile, whether in or outside the United States, if such legitimation takes place before the child reaches the age of eighteen years and the child is in the legal custody of the legitimating parent or parents at the time of such legitimation;

(D) a child born out of wedlock, by, through whom, or on whose behalf a status, privilege, or benefit is sought by virtue of the relationship of the child to its natural mother or to its natural father if the father has or had a bona fide parent-child relationship with the person;

(E) a child adopted while under the age of sixteen years if the child has been in the legal custody of, and has resided with, the adopting parent or parents for at least two years: Provided, That no natural parent of any such adopted child shall thereafter, by virtue of such parentage, be accorded any right, privilege, or status under this Act; or

(F) a child, under the age of sixteen at the time a petition is filed in his behalf to accord a classification as an immediate relative under section 201(b), who is an orphan because of the death or disappearance of, abandonment or desertion by, or separation or loss from, both parents, or for whom the sole or surviving parent is incapable of providing the proper care and has in writing irrevocably released the child for emigration and adoption; who has been adopted abroad by a United States citizen and spouse jointly, or by an unmarried United States citizen at least twenty-five years of age, who personally saw and observed the child prior to or during the adoption proceedings; or who is coming to the United States for adoption by a United States citizen and spouse jointly, or by an unmarried United States citizen at least twenty-five years of age, who have or has complied with the preadoption requirements, if any, of the child's proposed residence: Provided, That the Attorney General is satisfied that proper care will be furnished the child if admitted to the United States: Provided further, That no natural parent or prior adoptive parent of any such child shall thereafter, by virtue of such parentage, be accorded any right, privilege, or status under this Act.

The child must also be unmarried, dependent, and a minor. Unmarried means not married at the time of application for TD status. It does not matter if the child was previously married.[2] A minor is a child under the age of 21 years. Once a child who has TD status marries, becomes independent of the TN parent, or reaches the age of 21 that child is no longer entitled to TD status. The child should immediately leave the United States or obtain a valid immigration status. An employer will not be tracking the lives of its TN employees but may want to include this information in an information package it provides for all TN employees so they can be aware of it and not allow their children to get out of status. Since the passage of the Immigration Reform Act of 1996 the consequences of staying in the United States after lawful status has expired are much more severe.

Family members who are entitled to TD status do not include other relatives who are living in the TN professional's household, such as in-laws or nieces and nephews. Same sex partners are also excluded.

Citizenship of TD Family

While there is a strict requirement that a TN professional be a *citizen* of Canada or Mexico, there is no such requirement for the spouse or children who may obtain TD status. If the TD family member is not a citizen of Canada, they will require a valid passport and visa, unlike Canadian citizens who don't require a passport to enter the United States unless they are arriving from a location outside the Western Hemisphere.

Change of Status

It is possible for a family member who already has another nonimmigrant status in the United States to change to a TD status. For example, a child may be on a student visa (F-1 or M-1) in the United States when the parent is hired as a TN professional. If that child wants to change their status from a student visa to TD, he or she must file INS form I-539 at the Northern Service Center while they are in the United States. The child must file this far enough in advance so it will be processed and the new TD status granted before the student status expires. If the student status expires before the new TD status is granted the child will be out of status and be required to leave the United States. To reenter, he or she will have to make an application at a port of entry if the TN professional parent is Canadian, or at a U.S. Consulate if the TN professional parent is Mexican.

Extension of Stay

When the TN professional applies for an extension of stay, all the TD family members may apply for a similar extension of their TD status. Each TN and TD is valid for a period of one year. If family members did not all arrive on the same date, they will not have exactly the same issuance date; however, they will all have the same expiry date as the TN professional since their status is derived from the professional. When family members want to extend their stay for a subsequent year, they can each apply for a further twelve-month or shorter period to correspond with that of the TN professional.

Family members must be physically present in the United States at the time the application to extend their stay is filed. If the TD family members are applying for an extension of stay at the same time as the TN professional, each family member must file an INS form I-539 along with the INS form I-129 for the TN professional at the Northern Service Center. Each form I-539 must be accompanied by the appropriate filing fee.

If a family member is applying for an extension of stay at a different time than the TN professional, he or she must provide a copy of both sides of the TN professional's I-94 to establish that his or her spouse or parent is maintaining that valid nonimmigrant status. This must be filed with the INS form I-539 and the required fee at the Northern Service Center.

CANADIAN TD PROCEDURE

The procedure for a family member of a Canadian TN professional making an initial application for a TD status is similar to that for a Canadian citizen applying for TN status. The family member can apply with the TN professional at a port of entry, at a U.S. airport handling international traffic, or at a U.S. pre-clearance/pre-flight station. No prior petition is required. The family member must present documentation to show he or she is related to the TN professional as a spouse or unmarried minor child. If the TN application of the professional is approved, the accompanying family members will be granted TD status and issued an I-94.

If the family members are following to join a TN professional who has already been granted TN status and who is already living in the United States, they may make an application at a port of entry, at a U.S. airport handling international traffic, or at a U.S. pre-clearance/pre-flight station. Again no prior petition is required. The family member must present a copy of both sides of the TN professional's valid I-94 showing the TN status and evidence of the relationship to the TN person.

Family members who are not Canadian citizens will be required to present a valid passport to obtain TD status and to enter the United States. If the family member is a citizen of a British Commonwealth country holding landed status in Canada and has valid evidence of this, or if the non-Canadian citizen family member is visa exempt, they will not require a visa. Family members who are citizens of other countries will require a valid nonimmigrant visa classifying them as TD. Any documents that are not in English must be presented with an English translation. When presenting documents to the immigration officer, family members should have their originals and present a good photocopy for the immigration officer to keep. They should take a separate package for each family member who is applying. This will help make the process easier for the officer, who otherwise will have to take the time to photocopy all the documents.

There is no fee for the initial issuance of TD status or for an extension of TD status applied for at a port of entry or airport. However, there is a fee for an extension applied for from within the United States using form I-539.

MEXICAN TD PROCEDURE

When the Mexican citizen TN professional receives an approved Form I-129 granting TN status it must be presented at a U.S. Consulate. The family members may apply at the consulate at the same time as the TN professional for their TD status. The family members must present a valid passport and documentary evidence showing the relationship as spouse or child. Applicants should take original documents plus a complete photocopy with English translations for each family member to give to the consular official. Each family member will be issued a visa and an I-94 with their TD status and expiration date.

If family members want to apply for TD status after the TN professional has already received TN status and moved to the United States, they must take a valid passport, documents showing family relationship, and a photocopy of both sides of the TN professional's valid I-94 and apply at a U.S. Consulate.

EMPLOYER PROCEDURE AND POLICY

As an employer, you may want to provide a complete service to assist your TN professional employee to get their family TD status, or you may decide to provide only minimal information.

Initial Application

A company must participate in the process to obtain TN status for its professional Canadian and Mexican citizen employees. The minimum participation only requires writing a letter offering employment. Some companies may guide the employee through all the steps involved. Each TN employee should be given a minimum list of documents and procedures for obtaining TD status for his or her family members. This list should include the following list of documents and information to provide to the INS officer:

Birth certificates, with English translation if required.

Marriage certificate, with English translation if required.

Valid passport for each person (recommended for Canadian citizens as well).

Copy of TN professional's I-94.

Extension of Stay

A company may provide assistance for TN employee families in undertaking their immigration procedures. If a company does not want to get involved in assisting with this legal work because it does not have the resources or because very few TN employees are hired, it could provide basic information to the TN employees so they can do it themselves. Information that could be given out to employees includes

Toll-free telephone number to obtain INS forms.

Copies of INS form I-539 with instructions.

Address of INS Nebraska Service Center.

Photocopies of TN professional's I-94 (both sides).

Recommendation to maintain a valid passport and apply for renewals as necessary.

Advising TN Families

A company may want to alert its TN professional employees to some of the issues that may affect the status of their family members. A memo addressed to all TN employees could briefly review the law, policies, or procedure concerning such topics as

Effect of termination of TN professional's job on TD status of family.

Child who will become 21 years of age within twelve months of issuance of TD status.

Marriage of child in TD status.

Divorce of TN professional.

Birth of child while in the United States.

NOTES

1. INA § 101(a)(35).
2. INA, § 101(a)(39).

Part IV

Supplementary Issues

Chapter 11

Effect of a Strike

Concerns of organized labor in all three parties resulted in special provisions in NAFTA concerning strikes. Under NAFTA, a Party may refuse to issue an immigration document authorizing employment to a business person, where the temporary entry of that person might adversely affect the settlement of any labor dispute that is in progress at the place or intended place of employment or the employment of any person who is involved in such a dispute.

The United States enacted this protection for organized labor in regards to Mexican and Canadian citizens entering as traders and investors, intracompany transferees, and professionals. This provision does not include the temporary entry of business persons, since they are not employed in the United States. An alien who is a citizen of Canada or Mexico who seeks to enter the United States under NAFTA, will not be classified as a nonimmigrant with work authorization if there is in progress a strike or lockout in the course of a labor dispute in the occupational classification at the place or intended place of employment, unless the alien establishes that his or her entry will not adversely affect the settlement of the strike or lockout or the employment of any person who is involved in the strike or lockout.[1]

For a labor dispute to result in the denial or suspension of an E, L, or TN authorization, it must be a strike or other labor dispute involving work stoppage that is certified to by the U.S. Secretary of Labor or that was the subject of a communication from the Secretary of Labor to the Commissioner of Immigration and Naturalization. A consular officer will deny an application for E, L, or TN status when there is notice of a strike or other labor dispute involving a work stoppage. If an approval has been granted, but the alien has either not yet entered the United States or has entered but not yet commenced employment, the approval of the application can be suspended. If a strike or other labor dispute that involves a work stoppage is not certified, or the INS has not otherwise been informed by the Secretary of Labor that the strike or labor dispute is in progress, a consular officer will not deny a petition, suspend an approved petition, or deny entry to an applicant for TN status.

An alien seeking entry with E, L, or TN status for employment with an employer that is involved in a strike or lockout may demonstrate that his or her entry and employment will not adversely affect the settlement of the strike or lockout or the employment of any person who is involved. What evidence will be necessary to establish this will depend on the requirements of the employer, the job description of the E, L, or TN alien, and the category of employees on strike or lockout.

This procedure is complaint-driven. The DOL must be notified of the strike or labor dispute and be informed that it will affect the occupational classification of the person who is seeking temporary employment status under NAFTA. This complaint may come from a worker who sees the LCA notice posted for a TN employee. However, this posting requirement is only for Mexican citizens. The DOL must then certify that the requisite adverse conditions exist and notify consular officers. Without this certification from DOL, consular officers have no authority to refuse a visa based on a labor dispute. Without receiving a certification of a labor dispute, consular officers will assume labor dispute conditions do not exist and process applications according to the standard procedures.[2]

If the alien has already commenced employment in the United States and is participating in a strike or other labor dispute involving a work stoppage of workers, whether or not the strike or other labor dispute has been certified by the DOL, or whether the INS has been otherwise informed that such a strike or labor dispute is in progress, the alien will not be considered to be failing to maintain his or her status solely on account of past, present, or future participation in a strike or other labor dispute involving a work stoppage of workers. However, if the employee has commenced work when a strike or labor dispute occurs, and he or she participates in the work stoppage, this is not a failure to maintain status, and the TN alien will remain subject to all provisions relating to that status. The status and authorized period of stay will not be modified or extended because of any such work stoppage. Participation in a strike or labor dispute will not be grounds for deportation, but if the alien remains in the United States after his or her authorized period of stay it will be grounds for deportation.

Companies may decide to include a statement in a letter for a professional seeking TN status that there is no strike or labor dispute anticipated or occurring, or that there is no organized labor organization at the business, or some similar comment to help remove this issue as one of the considerations for the consular officer or free trade officer.

NOTES

1. North American Free Trade Agreement Implementation Act, Pub.L. 103-182, 107 Stat.2057, Dec. 8, 1993, § 3412(b), see Appendix D. Also see 8 CFR § 214.2(e)(3), 8 CFR § 214.2(l)(18), and 8 CFR § 214.6(k).

2. State Department Cable, Dec. 1993, Ref: State 367163.

Chapter 12

Changing the NAFTA Employee's Status to Permanent Resident

NAFTA does not contain any provisions about citizens from one Party obtaining permanent residence in another Party; it only deals with temporary employment. However, many people want to obtain permanent residence in the United States, either as their first goal or after having lived and worked for a period of time in the American system. This chapter will examine how employees who obtain a temporary work status under NAFTA can gain employment-based permanent residence in the United States. It will outline the categories of permanent residence that may be available for the four categories of NAFTA nonimmigrants.

BUSINESS PERSONS

There are no direct categories of permanent residence for business visitors. They may, however, depending on their individual education, skills, job, and family relationships, meet the requirements for one or more of the categories set out in the INA.

TRADERS AND INVESTORS

The visa for investors is generally called the Million Dollar Visa. Employment creation visas are for qualified immigrants seeking to enter the United States for the purpose of engaging in a new commercial enterprise that the alien has established, in which such alien has invested (after the date of the enactment of the Immigration Act of 1990), or is actively in the process of investing capital of not less than the amount specified in the INA, which will benefit the U.S. economy and create full-time employment for not fewer than ten U.S. citizens, aliens lawfully admitted for permanent residence, or other immigrants lawfully authorized to be employed in the United States (other than the immigrant and the immigrant's spouse, or children). In brief, the alien must invest $1 million in a business that will employ ten Americans.

Not less than 3,000 of the visas made available under this paragraph of the law in each fiscal year will be reserved for qualified immigrants who establish a new commercial enterprise by investment and which will create employment in a targeted employment area. The term "targeted employment area" means a rural area or an area that, at the time of the investment, has experienced high unemployment (of at least 150 percent of the national average rate). The term "rural area" means any area, other than an area within a metropolitan statistical area or within the outer boundary of any city or town, with a population of 20,000 or more (based on the most recent decennial census of the United States).

The amount of capital required for the new commercial enterprise is $1 million. The Attorney General, in consultation with the Secretary of Labor and the Secretary of State, may from time to time prescribe regulations increasing the dollar amount specified. This amount can be reduced to half for targeted employment areas and increased for high employment areas.

Very few applications are made for this category of permanent residence because the requirements are very strict, the permanent residence is conditionally granted for only two years, and the applicant must prove that all requirements have been met within two years to have the conditions removed.

INTRACOMPANY TRANSFEREE

A company may have an intracompany transferee who obtained L-1 status under NAFTA and want to keep that person at the U.S. office on a permanent basis. Likewise, a company may want to bring a citizen of Canada or Mexico to its U.S. office as a permanent employee to start with, and not seek a temporary status first. NAFTA does not contain any provisions about permanent immigration; however, the INA has provisions that allow certain multinational executives and managers to obtain permanent residence.[1]

Permanent residence for intracompany transferees, unlike the availability of L-1 status, is limited to certain executives and managers only, and is not available for employees with specialized knowledge. The employees who qualify must be employed in an executive or managerial capacity.[2] "Executive capacity" means an assignment within an organization in which the employee primarily

1. Directs the management of the organization or a major component or function of the organization;

2. Establishes the goals and policies of the organization, component, or function;

3. Exercises wide latitude in discretionary decision making; and

4. Receives only general supervision or direction from higher-level executives, the board of directors, or stockholders of the organization.

"Managerial capacity" means an assignment within an organization in which the employee primarily

1. Manages the organization, or a department, subdivision, function, or component of the organization;

2. Supervises and controls the work of other supervisory, professional, or managerial employees, or manages an essential function within the organization, or a department or subdivision of the organization;

3. If another employee or other employees are directly supervised, has the authority to hire and fire or recommend those as well as to perform other personnel actions (such as promotion and leave authorization), or if no other employee is directly supervised, functions at a senior level within the organizational hierarchy or with respect to the function managed; and

4. Exercises direction over the day-to-day operations of the activity or function for which the employee has authority.

An important issue in the petition is determining the managerial or executive capacities of the foreign employee. A first-line supervisor is not considered to be acting in a managerial capacity merely by virtue of his or her supervisory duties unless the employees supervised are professional. If staffing levels are used as a factor in determining whether an individual is acting in a managerial or executive capacity, the reasonable needs of the organization, component, or function, in light of the overall purpose and stage of development of the organization, component, or function, will be taken into account. An individual will not be considered to be acting in a managerial or executive capacity merely on the basis of the number of employees that the individual supervises or has supervised, or directs or has directed.

The qualifications for employers are also slightly different from those employers who petition for an L-1 visa and may include a parent, branch, affiliate, or subsidiary. Those who may apply for permanent residence for an intracompany transferee include

1. A firm or corporation, or other legal entity, or an affiliate or subsidiary of such a firm, corporation or other legal entity, if the alien is outside the United States, or

2. A firm or corporation or other legal entity, or an affiliate or subsidiary thereof, for which the alien is already working in the United States.

3. A prospective employer in the United States who is the same employer, or a subsidiary or affiliate of the firm or corporation or other legal entity that employed the alien overseas.

The following entities are considered to be affiliates:

1. One of two subsidiaries, both of which are owned and controlled by the same parent or individual;

2. One of two legal entities owned and controlled by the same group of individuals, each individual owning and controlling approximately the same share or proportion of each entity; or

3. A partnership that is organized outside the United States to provide accounting services, along with managerial or consulting services, and markets its accounting services under an internationally recognized name in an agreement with a worldwide coordinating organization that is owned and controlled by the member accounting firms, which include a U.S. partnership. The non-U.S. partnership in this case is considered to be an affiliate of the U.S. partnership if it markets its accounting services under the same internationally recognized name under the agreement with the worldwide coordinating organization of which the U.S. partnership is also a member.

"Subsidiary" means a firm, corporation, or other legal entity of which a parent owns, directly or indirectly, more than half of the entity and controls the entity; or owns, directly or indirectly, half of the entity and controls the entity; or owns, directly or indirectly, half of a 50–50 joint venture and has equal control and veto power over the entity; or owns, directly or indirectly, less than half of the entity, but in fact controls the entity.

The U.S. employer may file a petition on form I-140 for a multinational executive or manager for permanent residence. This petition must be accompanied by a statement from an authorized official of the petitioning U.S. employer that demonstrates that

1. If the employee is outside the United States, in the three years immediately preceding the filing of the petition, he or she has been employed outside the United States for at least one year in a managerial or executive capacity by a firm or corporation, or other legal entity, or by an affiliate or subsidiary of such a firm or corporation or other legal entity; or

2. If the employee is already in the United States working for the same employer or a subsidiary or affiliate of the firm or corporation, or other legal entity by which the employee was employed overseas, in the three years preceding entry as a nonimmigrant, the employee was employed by the entity abroad for at least one year in a managerial or executive capacity;

3. The prospective employer in the United States is the same employer or a subsidiary or affiliate of the firm or corporation or other legal entity by which the employee was employed overseas; and

4. The prospective United States employer has been doing business for at least one year.

The employer must also provide any additional evidence requested by the INS.

No labor certification is required for this classification; however, the prospective employer in the United States must furnish a job offer in the form of a statement that indicates that the employee is to be employed in the United States in a managerial or executive capacity. This letter must clearly describe the duties to be performed by the employee to show that the job comes within the requirements of managerial or executive capacity.

The approval of a permanent labor certification or the filing of a preference petition for an employee will not be a basis for denying an L petition, a request to extend an L petition, or the employee's application for admission, change of status, or extension of stay. The employee may legitimately come to the United States as a nonimmigrant under the L classification and depart voluntarily at the end of his or her authorized stay and, at the same time, lawfully seek to become a permanent resident of the United States.

PROFESSIONALS

There are a number of permanent residence categories available for professionals, including aliens of extraordinary ability, outstanding professors and researchers, members of the professions holding advanced degrees, aliens of exceptional ability, and professionals. Each of these is defined in the INA.[3]

"Aliens with extraordinary ability" is defined as follows: the alien has extraordinary ability in the sciences, arts, education, business, or athletics, which has been demonstrated by sustained national or international acclaim; the alien's achievements have been recognized in the field through extensive documentation; the alien seeks to enter the United States to continue work in the area of extraordinary ability; and the alien's entry into the United States will substantially benefit prospectively the United States.

"Outstanding professors and researchers" is defined as follows: the alien is recognized internationally as outstanding in a specific academic area; the alien has at least three years of experience in teaching or research in the academic area; the alien seeks to enter the United States for a tenured position (or tenure-track position) within a university or institution of higher education to teach in the academic area, for a comparable position with a university or institution of higher education to conduct research in the area, or for a comparable position to conduct research in the area with a department, division, or institute of a private employer, if the department, division, or institute employs at least three persons full time in research activities; and the alien has achieved documented accomplishments in an academic field.

"Members of the professions holding advanced degrees or their equivalent" are aliens who, because of their exceptional ability in the sciences, arts, or business, will substantially benefit prospectively the national economy, cultural or educational interests, or welfare of the United States, and whose services in the sciences, arts, professions, or business are sought by an employer in the United States. In determining whether an immigrant has "exceptional ability," the possession of a degree, diploma, certificate, or similar award from a college, university, school, or other institution of learning; or a license to practice, or certification for, a particular profession or occupation, shall not by itself be considered sufficient evidence of such exceptional ability.

"Professionals" are qualified immigrants who hold a baccalaureate degree and who are members of the professions.

Procedure

The procedure to apply for permanent residence starts with the employer, or in some cases the alien, filing a petition on INS form I-140 and supporting documentation with the INS Service Center for the location of the employment. Initial evidence must be attached in the supporting documents. Usually, ordinary legible photocopies of documents (except for labor certifications from the Department of Labor) will be acceptable for initial filing and approval. However, in some cases the INS will require original documents. Evidence relating to qualifying experience or training must be in the form of letter(s) from current or former employer(s) or trainer(s) and must include the name, address, and title of the writer, and a specific description of the duties performed by the alien or of the training received. If such evidence is unavailable, other documentation relating to the alien's experience or training can be submitted. Any petition filed by or for an employment-based immigrant that requires an offer of employment must be accompanied by evidence that the prospective U.S. employer has the ability to pay the offered wage. The petitioner must demonstrate this ability at the time the priority date is established and until the beneficiary obtains lawful permanent residence. Evidence of this ability must be either in the form of copies of annual reports, federal tax returns, or audited financial statements. In a case where the prospective U.S. employer employs 100 or more workers, the INS may accept a statement from a financial officer of the organization that establishes the prospective employer's ability to pay the proffered wage. In appropriate cases, additional evidence, such as profit-loss statements, bank account records, or personnel records, may be submitted by the petitioner or requested by the INS.

Aliens with Extraordinary Ability

An alien, or any person on behalf of the alien, may file an I-140 visa petition for classification as an alien of extraordinary ability in the sciences, arts, education, business, or athletics. "Extraordinary ability" means a level of expertise indicating that the individual is one of that small percentage who have risen to the very top of the field of endeavor.

A petition for an alien of extraordinary ability must be accompanied by evidence that the alien has sustained national or international acclaim and that his or her achievements have been recognized in the field of expertise. Such evidence shall include documentation of a one-time achievement (that is, a major, international recognized award), or at least three of the following:

1. Documentation of the alien's receipt of lesser nationally or internationally recognized prizes or awards for excellence in the field of endeavor;

2. Documentation of the alien's membership in associations in the field for which classification is sought, which require outstanding achievements of their members, as judged by recognized national or international experts in their disciplines or fields;

3. Published material about the alien in professional or major trade publications or other major media, relating to the alien's work in the field for which classification is sought. Such evidence shall include the title, date, and author of the material, and any necessary translation;

4. Evidence of the alien's participation, either individually or on a panel, as a judge of the work of others in the same or an allied field of specification for which classification is sought;

5. Evidence of the alien's original scientific, scholarly, artistic, athletic, or business-related contributions of major significance in the field;

6. Evidence of the alien's authorship of scholarly articles in the field, in professional or major trade publications or other major media;

7. Evidence of the display of the alien's work in the field at artistic exhibitions or showcases;

8. Evidence that the alien has performed in a leading or critical role for organizations or establishments that have a distinguished reputation;

9. Evidence that the alien has commanded a high salary or other significantly high remuneration for services, in relation to others in the field; or

10. Evidence of commercial successes in the performing arts, as shown by box office receipts or record, cassette, compact disk, or video sales.

If the above standards do not readily apply to the beneficiary's occupation, the petitioner may submit comparable evidence to establish the beneficiary's eligibility.[4]

Neither an offer for employment in the United States nor a labor certification is required for this classification; however, the petition must be accompanied by clear evidence that the alien is coming to the United States to continue work in the area of expertise. Such evidence may include letter(s) from prospective employer(s), evidence of prearranged commitments such as contracts, or a statement from the beneficiary detailing plans on how he or she intends to continue his or her work in the United States.

Outstanding Professors and Researchers

Any U.S. employer desiring and intending to employ a professor or researcher who is outstanding in an academic field may file an I-140 visa petition for such classification.[5] Academic field means a body of specialized knowledge offered for study at an accredited U.S. university or institution of higher education. Permanent, in reference to a research position, means either tenured, tenure-track, or for a term of indefinite or unlimited duration, and in which the employee will ordinarily have an expectation of continued employment unless there is good cause for termination.

A petition for an outstanding professor or researcher must be accompanied by:

1. Evidence that the professor or researcher is recognized internationally as outstanding in the academic field specified in the petition. Such evidence must consist of at least two of the following:

(a) Documentation of the alien's receipt of major prizes or awards for outstanding achievement in the academic field;

(b) Documentation of the alien's membership in associations in the academic field that require outstanding achievements of their members;

(c) Published material in professional publications written by others about the alien's work in the academic field. Such material shall include the title, date, and author of the material, and any necessary translation;

(d) Evidence of the alien's participation, either individually or on a panel, as the judge of the work of others in the same or an allied academic field;

(e) Evidence of the alien's original scientific or scholarly research contributions to the academic field; or

(f) Evidence of the alien's authorship of scholarly books or articles (in scholarly journals with international circulation) in the academic field;

2. Evidence that the alien has at least three years of experience in teaching and/or research in the academic field. Experience in teaching or research while working on an advanced degree will only be acceptable if the alien has acquired the degree, and if the teaching duties were such that he or she had full responsibility for the class taught, or if the research conducted toward the degree has been recognized within the academic field as outstanding. Evidence of teaching and/or research experience

shall be in the form of letter(s) from current or former employer(s) and shall include the name, address, and title of the writer, and a specific description of the duties performed by the alien; and

3. An offer of employment from a prospective U.S. employer. A labor certification is not required for this classification. The offer of employment shall be in the form of a letter from:

(a) A U.S. university or institution of higher learning offering the alien a tenured or tenure-track teaching position in the alien's academic field;

(b) A U.S. university or institution of higher learning offering the alien a permanent research position in the alien's academic field; or

(c) A department, division, or institute of a private employer offering the alien a permanent research position in the alien's academic field. The department, division, or institute must demonstrate that it employs at least three persons full time in research positions, and that it has achieved documented accomplishments in an academic field.

Aliens Who Are Members of the Professions Holding Advanced Degrees or Aliens of Exceptional Ability

Any U.S. employer may file a petition on form I-140 for classification of an alien as an alien who is a member of the professions holding an advanced degree or an alien of exceptional ability in the sciences, arts, or business. If an alien is claiming exceptional ability in the sciences, arts, or business and is seeking an exemption from the requirement of a job offer in the United States, then the alien, or anyone on the alien's behalf, may be the petitioner.[6]

Advanced degree means any U.S. academic or professional degree, or a foreign equivalent degree above that of baccalaureate. A U.S. Baccalaureate Degree or a foreign equivalent degree followed by at least five years of progressive experience in the specialty shall be considered the equivalent of a Master's Degree. If a Doctoral Degree is customarily required by the specialty, the alien must have a U.S. Doctorate or a foreign equivalent degree. "Exceptional ability in the sciences, arts, or business" means a degree of expertise significantly above that ordinarily encountered in the sciences, arts, or business. "Profession" means one of the occupations listed in the INA (architects, engineers, lawyers, physicians, surgeons, and teachers), as well as any occupation for which a U.S. baccalaureate degree or its foreign equivalent is the minimum requirement for entry into the occupation.

The petition must be accompanied by documentation showing that the alien is a professional holding an advanced degree or an alien of exceptional ability in the sciences, the arts, or business.

1. To show that the alien is a professional holding an advanced degree, the petition must be accompanied by:

(a) An official academic record showing that the alien has a U.S. advanced degree or a foreign equivalent degree; or

(b) An official academic record showing that the alien has a U.S. Baccalaureate Degree or a foreign equivalent degree, and evidence in the form of letters from current or former employer(s) showing that the alien has at least five years of progressive post-baccalaureate experience in the specialty.

2. To show that the alien is an alien of exceptional ability in the sciences, arts, or business, the petition must be accompanied by at least three of the following:

(a) An official academic record showing that the alien has a degree, diploma, certificate, or similar award from a college, university, school, or other institution of learning relating to the area of exceptional ability;

(b) Evidence in the form of letter(s) from current or former employer(s) showing that the alien has at least ten years of full-time experience in the occupation for which he or she is being sought;

(c) A license to practice the profession or certification for a particular profession or occupation;

(d) Evidence that the alien has commanded a salary, or other remuneration for services, which demonstrates exceptional ability;

(e) Evidence of membership in professional associations; or

(f) Evidence of recognition for achievements and significant contributions to the industry or field by peers, governmental entities, or professional or business organizations.

3. If the above standards do not readily apply to the beneficiary's occupation, the petitioner may submit comparable evidence to establish the beneficiary's eligibility.

Every petition must be accompanied by an individual labor certification from the U.S. Department of Labor, by an application for Schedule A designation (if applicable), or by documentation to establish that the alien qualifies for one of the shortage occupations in the Department of Labor's Labor Market Information Pilot Program. However, it is possible to obtain an exemption from a job offer for this category. The INS may exempt the requirement of a job offer, and thus of a labor certification, for aliens of exceptional ability in the sciences, arts, or business if exemption would be in the national interest. To apply for the exemption, the petitioner must submit form ETA-750B, *Statement of Qualifications of Alien*, in duplicate, as well as evidence to support the claim that such exemption would be in the national interest. The documentation that demonstrates how this person's presence in the United States will be in the national interest is unique to each alien, and usually such documentation is extensive.

Professionals

Any U.S. employer may file a petition on form I-140 for classification of an alien as a professional.[7] "Professional" means a qualified alien who holds at least a U.S. Baccalaureate Degree or a foreign equivalent degree and who is a member of the professions. This category requires a labor certification, which is a document from the DOL that acknowledges that there are no qualified U.S. workers who could fill the job. Obtaining a labor certification can take up to two years, and involves filing an application with the state and federal DOL, advertising the job according to DOL specifications, interviewing or assessing all applicants, and reporting to the DOL why each applicant was not suitable. The labor certification will be denied if any alien applicant was minimally qualified for the job, if the job description appears to be tailored to the education and skills of the alien, if all applicants were not interviewed, or if the job application was deficient.

The petitioner employer must file as initial evidence with the form I-140

1. An individual labor certification from the Department of Labor, an application for Schedule A designation, or documentation to establish that the alien qualifies for one of the shortage occupations in the Department of Labor's Labor Market Information Pilot Program. The job offer portion of an individual labor certification, Schedule A application, or Pilot Program application for a professional must demonstrate that the job requires the minimum of a Baccalaureate Degree.

2. Evidence of training or experience, which must be supported by letters from trainers or employers giving the name, address, and title of the trainer or employer, and a description of the training received or the experience of the alien.

3. Evidence that the alien holds a U.S. Baccalaureate Degree or a foreign equivalent degree and evidence that the alien is a member of the professions. Evidence of a Baccalaureate Degree shall be in the form of an official college or university record showing the date the Baccalaureate Degree was awarded and the area of concentration of study. To show that the alien is a member of the professions, the petitioner must submit evidence showing that the minimum of a Baccalaureate Degree is required for entry into the occupation.

NOTES

1. INA § 203(b)(1)(C).
2. INA § 203(b)(1)(C), and 8 C.F.R. § 204.5(j)(2).
3. INA § 203(b).
4. 8 C.F.R. § 204.5(h)(4).
5. 8 C.F.R. § 204.5(i)(2).
6. 8 C.F.R. § 204.5(k)(2).
7. 8 C.F.R. § 204.5(l)(2).

Chapter 13

Employer Obligations for Employment Eligibility

In its attempt to reduce illegal immigration, Congress drastically shifted the obligation for enforcement of the U.S. immigration laws to the employer under the Immigration Reform and Control Act of 1986. The act created a legal obligation for employers to verify the employment eligibility of all employees. The act made it unlawful for an employer to fail to fully comply with the strict requirements of verifying all employment eligibility and provided for severe fines and penalties. The rationale for the shift in obligations was that employment is often the magnet that attracts persons to come to, or stay in, the United States illegally. The purpose of the employer sanctions was to remove the magnet that draws illegal immigrants to the United States, by requiring the employer to hire only persons who may legally work in the United States. To comply with the law, the employer has to verify the identity and employment eligibility of each new hire by completing a form I-9. It was thought that if employers refused to hire unauthorized aliens, this would deter aliens from entering illegally or violating their status in search of employment.

The act does not obligate employers to comply with the requirements of completing form I-9 for employees hired before November 6, 1986 who continue to be employed with the same employer, however.

The employer is required to comply with the following:

1. Ensure that all employees hired after November 6, 1986 fill out Section 1 of the Form I-9 when they start work.
2. Review documentation establishing each employee's identity and eligibility to work.

3. Retain the form I-9 for three years after the date the person begins work, or one year after the person's employment is terminated, whichever is longer.

4. Make the form I-9 available for inspection to an officer of the INS, the DOL, or the Office of Special Counsel for Immigration Related Unfair Employment Practices (OSC) upon request. However, this does not preclude the INS, the DOL, or the OSC from obtaining warrants based on probable cause for entry onto the premises of suspected violators without advance notice.

INS Inspections

The INS will not barge in and demand a company's files unannounced. The INS must give an employer a minimum of three-days notice prior to making an inspection. If an employer receives a notice of inspection, during the time before the inspection the employer should make sure it has an I-9 form for each employee, correct any errors on the forms (according to permitted restrictions on making corrections), make a list of all employees, and make sure other relevant corporate and business documents are in order. The INS inspector will examine and take copies of the I-9 forms and other documents.

Some time after the inspection, the INS will send the employer one of three types of notices. A notice of compliance means everything is in order. A notice of deficiency will state what corrective actions must be undertaken. A notice that lists invalid or questionable alien employees will contain a warning that, if the employer continues to employ the named person, it could result in a fine. An employer must take immediate steps to comply with either of the last two notices. Further notices, hearings, and possible fines follow notices of deficiency or invalid employees. Upon receiving either of these notices, an employer should immediately contact an immigration or other attorney who has experience with this process because employers are subject to potential fines ranging up to $10,000 for each violation.

Anti-Discrimination Provisions

For the purpose of satisfying the employment eligibility verification requirements, an employer cannot request that an employee or prospective employee present more or different documents than are required by the law. An employer is also prohibited from refusing to honor documents that on their face reasonably appear to be genuine and to relate to the person presenting them. To violate these standards is deemed to be an unfair immigration-related employment practice.

Document Fraud Provisions

Employers, employees, and anyone assisting them will be operating unlawfully if they knowingly engage in any of the following activities for the purpose of satisfying a requirement of this act.

1. Forging, counterfeiting, altering, or falsely making any document.
2. Using, attempting to use, possessing, obtaining, accepting, or receiving any forged, counterfeit, altered, or falsely made documents.
3. Using or attempting to use any document lawfully issued to a person other than the possessor.
4. Accepting or receiving any document unlawfully issued to a person other than the possessor for the purpose of complying with the employment eligibility requirements.

WHEN TO COMPLETE FORM I-9

Form I-9 must be completed any time an employer hires someone to perform labor or services in return for wages or other remuneration. A form I-9 does not have to be completed for the following groups:

1. Persons hired before November 7, 1986, who are continuing in their employment and have a reasonable expectation of continuing employment.
2. Persons employed for casual domestic work in a private home on a sporadic, irregular, or intermittent basis.
3. Persons who are independent contractors.
4. Persons who provide labor who are employed by a contractor providing contract services.

An employer cannot call an alien an independent contractor if the employer knows the alien is not allowed to work in the United States.

HOW TO COMPLETE FORM I-9

Employees must complete Section 1 at the time they begin work by filling in the correct information and signing and dating the form. The employer is responsible for reviewing each I-9 to ensure that it has been fully and properly completed. In Section 2, the employee must provide to the employer an original document or documents that establish identity and employment eligibility within three business days of the date employment begins. Some documents establish both identity and employment eligibility. Other documents establish identity only, or employment eligibility only. Employees can choose which document(s) they want to present from the lists of acceptable documents. The lists of acceptable documents and form I-9 appear in Appendix J.

The employer must examine the original document or documents presented and then fully complete section 2 of the form I-9. Upon examination of the document or documents, the employer must record the title, issuing authority, number, and expiration date of the document(s); fill in the date of hire and correct information in the certification block; and sign and date the form I-9. The employer must accept any document or combination of documents presented by the individual that reasonably appear on their face to be genuine and to relate to the person presenting them. The employer must not specify which documents an employee must present.

If an employee is unable to present the required document(s) within three business days of the date employment begins, the employee must present to the employer a receipt for the application for the document(s) within three business days. The employee must have indicated, by checking an appropriate box in Section 1, that he or she is already eligible to be employed in the United States. When an employee provides the employer with a receipt showing that he or she has applied for a document evidencing that eligibility, the employer should record the document title in Section 2 of form I-9 and write the word "receipt" and any document number in the document number space. The employee must present the actual document within 90 days of the date employment begins. At that time, the employer should cross out the word "receipt" and any accompanying document number, insert the number from the actual documents presented, and initial and date the change.

Future Expiration Dates

Future expiration dates may appear on the form I-9 or on the employment authorization documents of aliens, including among others, permanent residents, temporary residents, and refugees. The INS includes expiration dates even on documents issued to aliens with permanent work authorizations. The existence of a future expiration date does not preclude continuous employment authorization, nor does it mean that subsequent employment authorizations will not be granted. Because of this, the future expiration date should not be considered in determining whether the alien is qualified for a particular position.

Caution should be exhibited by employers where considerations of a future employment authorization expiration date in determining whether an alien is qualified for a particular job may constitute employment discrimination. Nonetheless, it is the employer's obligation to reverify the employee's eligibility to work when any expiration date on the form I-9 is reached.

Reverifying Employment Authorization for Current Employees

When an employee's work authorization expires, the employer must reverify the employee's employment eligibility. Section 3 of the form I-9 is specifically for the reverification of employment eligibility. If Section 3 has been previously used, then a new Form I-9 must be completed and kept with the original.

To maintain continuous employment eligibility, an employee with temporary work authorization should apply for a new work authorization at least 90 days before the current expiration date. If the INS fails to adjudicate the application for employment authorization within 90 days, then the employee will be authorized for a period not to exceed 240 days.

Reverifying or Updating Employment Authorization for Rehired Employees

When an employee is rehired, the employer must ensure that the employee is still authorized to work. This may be done by completing a new form I-9, or by updating the original I-9 by completing Section 3. Section 3 reverification can only be used if the employee being rehired is in fact rehired within three years of the initial date of hire, and the employee's previous grant of work authorization has expired, but he or she is currently eligible to work in a different capacity, or under a new grant of work authorization than the one covered in the original form I-9.

UNLAWFUL DISCRIMINATION

Current legislation makes it unlawful for employers of four or more employees to discriminate in hiring, firing, or recruiting on the basis of national origin or citizenship status. In this area of potential liability, the employer's actions are regulated not only by the INS but also by the DOL, the EEOC, and a multitude of Civil Rights Acts. In practice, this means that employers must treat all employees the same when completing the form I-9. Employers cannot set different employment eligibility verification standards or require that different documents be presented by different groups of employees. Employees can choose which documents they want to present from the lists of acceptable documents. An employer cannot request that an employee present more or different documents when the documents presented reasonably appear to be genuine and to relate to the person presenting them. An employer cannot refuse to accept a document, or refuse to hire an individual, because a document has a future expiration date. For example, temporary resident aliens have registrations cards, and persons granted asylum have INS work authorization documents that will expire, but they are ordinarily granted extensions of their employment authorization, and they are protected by law from discrimination.

Generally, employers who have four or more employees cannot limit jobs to U.S. citizens and exclude authorized aliens. Such limitations may only be applied to a specific position when required by law, regulation, or executive order; when required by a federal, state, or local government contract; or when the Attorney General determines that U.S. citizenship is essential for doing business with an agency or department of the federal, state or local government.

On an individual basis, an employer may legally prefer a U.S. citizen or national over an equally qualified alien to fill a specific position. However, an employer may not adopt a blanket policy of always preferring a qualified citizen over a qualified alien.

Verification of identity and employment eligibility is not required until an individual actually starts work. The form I-9 should be completed at the same point in the employment process for all employees. Different procedures should not be established based on an individual's appearance, name, accent, or other factors.

Procedures for Filing Complaints

Discrimination charges may be filed by an individual who believes he or she is the victim of employment discrimination, a person acting on behalf of such an individual, or an INS officer who has reason to believe that discrimination has occurred. Charges of national origin and citizenship status discrimination against employers can be filed with the OSC within the Department of Justice. Any discrimination charges filed must be done so within 180 days of the incident. Upon receipt of the charge, the OSC will notify the employer within ten days that the charges have been filed, and that an investigation will be conducted. If the OSC has not filed a complaint with an administrative law judge within 120 days of receiving a charge of discrimination, it will notify the person making the charge of its determination not to file a complaint.

An employer is prohibited from taking retaliatory action against a person who has filed a charge of discrimination or who was a witness, or otherwise participated in, the investigation of another person's complaint. Such retaliatory action is a violation of the anti-discrimination provisions of many federal regulations.

PENALTIES FOR PROHIBITED PRACTICES

Unlawful Employment

Employers determined to have knowingly hired unauthorized aliens may be ordered to cease and desist from such activity and pay a civil money penalty as follows:

1. First Offense. Not less than $250 and not more than $2,000 for each unauthorized alien.

2. Second Offense. Not less than $2,000 and not more than $5,000 for each unauthorized alien.

3. Subsequent Offenses. Not less than $3,000 and not more than $10,000 for each unauthorized alien.

After November 6, 1986, if an employer uses a contract, subcontract, or exchange entered into, renegotiated, or extended, to obtain the labor of an alien and knows the alien is not authorized to work in the United States, the employer will be considered to have knowingly hired an unauthorized alien. The employer will be subject to the penalties set out above.

Criminal penalties may be levied on employers who engage in a pattern or practice of knowingly hiring or continuing to employ unauthorized aliens. Emloyers who are convicted of this offense may be sentenced to up to six months of incarceration for each unauthorized alien employed. The court may also impose a fine of up to $3,000 for each offense in addition to, or instead of, imprisonment.

Unlawful Discrimination

Employers are also liable for unlawful discrimination in failing to hire aliens if an investigation reveals that an employer has engaged in unfair immigration-related employment practices under federal regulations. Upon such finding, an employer may be required to do any of the following actions:

1. Hire or reinstate, with or without back pay, individuals directly injured by the discrimination.

2. Lift any restrictions on an employee's assignments, work shifts, or movements.

3. Educate all personnel involved in the hiring process and in complying with the employer sanctions and anti-discrimination laws about the requirements of these laws.

4. Remove a false performance review or false warning from an employee's personnel file.

Employers may also be ordered to pay a civil money penalty as follows:

1. First Offense. Not less than $250 and not more than $2,000 for each individual discriminated against.

2. Second Offense. Not less than $2000 and not more than $5,000 for each individual discriminated against.

3. Subsequent Offenses. Not less than $3,000 and not more than $10,000 for each individual discriminated against.

4. Unlawful Request for More or Different Documents. Not less than $100 and not more than $1,000 for each individual discriminated against.

Employers may also be ordered to keep certain records regarding the hiring of applicants and employees. The courts also have the right to award attorneys' fees to prevailing parties other than the United States.

HOW EMPLOYERS CAN PROTECT THEMSELVES

The employer should review its files and complete the documentation before a problem develops. It will be too late when an INS notice of inspection is received. There will not be enough time to bring the I-9 files up to date. Furthermore, an employer who makes corrections or completes documents after receiving an INS notice may be in violation of the law and subject to catch-up penalties. Do the documentation now. Employers would be well advised to get an immigration attorney to audit all I-9 records for deficiencies and potential problems. The attorney can also teach an employer how to complete and maintain I-9 and related records.

Appendixes

Appendix A

North American Free Trade Agreement, Chapter Sixteen, Temporary Entry for Business Persons

ARTICLE 1601: GENERAL PRINCIPLES

Further to Article 102 (Objectives), the provisions of this Chapter reflect the preferential trading relationship between the Parties, the desirability of facilitating temporary entry on a reciprocal basis and of establishing transparent criteria and procedures for temporary entry, and the need to ensure border security and protect the domestic labor force and permanent employment in their respective territories.

ARTICLE 1602: GENERAL OBLIGATIONS

1. Each Party shall apply its measures relating to the provisions of this Chapter in accordance with Article 1601, and in particular, shall apply expeditiously such measures so as to avoid unduly impairing or delaying trade in goods or services or conduct of investment activities under this Agreement.

2. The Parties shall endeavor to develop and adopt common criteria, definitions and interpretations for the implementations of this Chapter.

ARTICLE 1603: GRANT OF TEMPORARY ENTRY

1. Each Party shall grant, in accordance with this Chapter, including Annex 1603, temporary entry to business persons who are otherwise qualified for entry under applicable measures relating to public health and safety and national security.

2. A Party may refuse to issue an immigration document authorizing employment to a business person where the temporary entry of that person might affect adversely:

(a) the settlement of any labor dispute that is in progress at the place or intended place of employment; or

(b) the employment of any person who is involved in such dispute.

3. When a Party refuses pursuant to paragraph 2 to issue an immigration document authorizing employment, it shall:

(a) inform in writing the business person of the reasons for the refusal; and

(b) promptly notify in writing the Party whose business person has been refused entry of the reasons for the refusal.

4. Each Party shall limit any fees for processing applications for temporary entry of business persons to the approximate cost of services rendered.

ARTICLE 1604: PROVISION OF INFORMATION

1. Further to Article 1802 (Publication), each Party shall:

(a) provide to the other Parties such materials as will enable them to become acquainted with its measures relating to the provisions of this Chapter; and

(b) not later than one year after the date of entry into force of this Agreement, prepare, publish and make available in its own territory, and in the territories of the other Parties, explanatory material in a consolidated document regarding the requirements for temporary entry under this Chapter in such a manner as to enable business persons of the other Parties to become acquainted with them.

2. Subject to Annex 1604.2, each Party shall collect and maintain, and make available to the other Parties in accordance with its domestic law, data respecting the granting of temporary entry under this Chapter to business persons of the other Parties who have been issued immigration documentation, including that specific to each occupation, profession or activity.

ARTICLE 1605: WORKING GROUPS

1. The Parties hereby establish a Temporary Entry Working Group, comprising representatives of each Party, including immigration officials.

2. The Working Group shall meet at least once a year to consider:

(a) the implementation and administration of this Chapter;

(b) the development of measures to further facilitate temporary entry of business persons on a reciprocal basis;

(c) the waiving of labor certification tests or procedures of similar effect for spouses of business persons who have been granted temporary entry for more than one year under Sections B, C, or D of Annex 1603; and

(d) proposed modifications of or additions to this Chapter.

ARTICLE 1606: DISPUTE SETTLEMENT

A Party may not initiate proceedings under Article 2007 regarding a refusal to grant temporary entry under this Chapter or a particular case arising under Article 1602(1) unless:

(a) the matter involves a pattern of practice; and

(b) the business person has exhausted available administrative remedies regarding the particular matter, provided that such remedies shall be deemed to be exhausted if a final decision in the matter has not been issued by the competent authority within one year of the institution of an administrative proceeding, and the failure to issue a determination is not attributable to delay caused by the business person.

ARTICLE 1607: RELATIONSHIP TO OTHER CHAPTERS

Except for Chapter One (Objectives), Chapter Two (General Definitions), Chapter Twenty (Institutional Arrangements and Dispute Settlement), Chapter Twenty-Two (Final Provisions) and Articles 1801 through 1804, no provision of any other Chapter shall impose any obligation upon a Party regarding its immigration measures.

ARTICLE 1608: DEFINITIONS

For the purposes of this Chapter:

business person means a citizen of a Party who is engaged in the trade of goods, the provision of services or the conduct of investment activities;

citizen means "citizen" as defined in Annex 1608;

existing means "existing" as defined in Annex 1608; and

temporary entry means entry into the territory of a Party by a business person of another Party without the intent to establish permanent residence.

ANNEX 1603
TEMPORARY ENTRY FOR BUSINESS PERSONS

Section A—Business Visitors

1. Each Party shall grant temporary entry to a business person seeking to engage in a business activity set out in Schedule I, without requiring that person to obtain an employment authorization, provided that the business person otherwise complies with existing immigration measures applicable to temporary entry, upon presentation of:

(a) proof of citizenship of a Party;

(b) documentation demonstrating that the business person will be so engaged and describing the purpose of entry; and

(c) evidence demonstrating that the proposed business activity is international in scope and that the business person is not seeking to enter the local labor market.

2. Each Party shall provide that a business person may satisfy the requirements of paragraph 1(c) by demonstrating that:

(a) the primary source of remuneration for the proposed business activity is outside the territory of the Party granting temporary entry; and

(b) the business person's principal place of business and the actual place of accrual of profits, at least predominantly, remain outside such territory. A Party shall normally accept an oral declaration as to the principal place of business and the actual place of accrual of profits. If the Party requires further proof, it shall normally consider a letter from the employer attesting to these matters as sufficient proof.

3. Each Party shall grant temporary entry to a business person seeking to engage

in a business activity other than those set out in Schedule I, without requiring that person to obtain an employment authorization, on a basis no less favorable than that provided under the existing provisions of the measure set out in Appendix 1603.A, provided that the business person otherwise complies with existing immigration measures applicable to temporary entry.

4. No Party shall:

(a) as a condition for temporary entry under paragraph 1 or 3, require prior approval procedures, petitions, labor certification tests, or other procedures of similar effect; or

(b) impose or maintain any numerical restriction relating to temporary entry under paragraph 1 or 3.

5. Notwithstanding paragraph 4, a Party may require a business person seeking temporary entry under this Part to obtain a visa or its equivalent prior to entry. Before imposing a visa requirement, such Party shall consult with a Party whose business persons would be affected with a view to avoiding the imposition of the requirement. With respect to an existing visa requirement, a Party shall, at the request of a Party whose business persons are subject to the requirement, consult with that Party with a view to its removal.

Section B—Traders and Investors

1. Each Party shall grant temporary entry and provide confirming documentation to a business person seeking to:

(a) carry on substantial trade in goods or services principally between the territory of the Party of which the business person is a citizen and the territory of the Party into which entry is sought; or

(b) establish, develop, administer or provide advice or key technical services to the operation of an investment to which the business person or the business person's enterprise had committed, or is in the process of committing, a substantial amount of capital, in a capacity that is supervisory, executive or involves essential skills, provided that the business person otherwise complies with existing immigration measures applicable to temporary entry.

2. No Party shall:

(a) as a condition for temporary entry under paragraph 1, require labor certification tests or other procedures of similar effect; or

(b) impose or maintain any numerical restrictions relating to temporary entry under paragraph 1.

3. Notwithstanding paragraph 2, a Party may require a business person seeking temporary entry under this Part to obtain a visa or its equivalent prior to entry.

Section C—Intra-Company Transferees

1. Each Party shall grant temporary entry and provide confirming documentation to a business person employed by an enterprise who seeks to render services to that enterprise or a subsidiary or affiliate thereof, in a capacity that is managerial, executive, or involves specialized knowledge, provided that the business person otherwise complies with existing immigration measures applicable to temporary entry.

A Party may require that such business person shall have been employed continuously by such enterprise for one year within the three-year period immediately preceding the date of the application for admission.

2. No Party shall:

(a) as a condition for temporary entry under paragraph 1, require labor certification tests or other procedures of similar effect; or

(b) impose or maintain any numerical restrictions relating to temporary entry under paragraph 1.

3. Notwithstanding paragraph 2, a Party may require a business person seeking temporary entry under this Part to obtain a visa or its equivalent prior to entry. Before imposing a visa requirement, such Party shall consult with a Party whose business persons would be affected with a view to avoiding the imposition of the requirement. With respect to an existing visa requirement, a Party shall, at the request of a Party whose business persons are subject to the requirement, consult with that Party with a view to its removal.

Section D—Professionals

1. Each Party shall grant temporary entry and provide confirming documentation to a business person seeking to engage in a business activity at a professional level in a profession set out in Schedule II, if the business person otherwise complies with existing immigration measures applicable to temporary entry, upon presentation of:

(a) proof of citizenship of a Party; and

(b) documentation demonstrating that the business person will be so engaged and describing the purpose of entry.

2. No Party shall:

(a) as a condition for temporary entry under paragraph 1, require prior approval procedures, petitions, labor certification tests, or other procedures of similar effect; or

(b) impose or maintain any numerical restriction relating to temporary entry under paragraph 1.

3. Notwithstanding paragraph 2, a Party may require a business person seeking temporary entry under this Part to obtain a visa or its equivalent prior to entry. Before imposing a visa requirement, such Party shall consult with a Party whose business persons would be affected with a view to avoiding the imposition of the requirement. With respect to an existing visa requirement, a Party shall, at the request of a Party whose business persons are subject to the requirement, consult with that Party with a view to its removal.

4. Notwithstanding paragraphs 1 and 2, a Party may establish an annual numerical limit, which shall be set out in Schedule III, regarding temporary entry of business persons of another Party seeking to engage in business activities at a professional level in a profession set out in Schedule II, if the Parties concerned have not agreed otherwise prior to the entry into force of this Agreement for such Parties. In establishing such a limit, such Party shall consult with the other Party concerned.

5. A Party establishing a numerical limit pursuant to paragraph 4, unless the Parties concerned agree otherwise:

(a) shall, for each year after the first year after the date of entry into force of this

Agreement, consider increasing the numerical limit set out in Schedule III by an amount to be established in consultation with the other Party concerned, taking into account the demand for temporary entry under this Part;

(b) shall not apply its procedures established pursuant to paragraph 1 to the temporary entry of a business person subject to the numerical limit, but may require such business person to comply with its other procedures applicable to the temporary entry of professionals; and

(c) may, in consultation with the other Party concerned, grant temporary entry under paragraph 1 to a business person who practices in a profession where accreditation, licensing, and certification requirements are mutually recognized by such Parties.

6. Nothing in paragraphs 4 or 5 shall be construed so as to limit the ability of a business person to seek temporary entry under a Party's applicable immigration measures relating to the entry of professionals other than those adopted or maintained pursuant to paragraph 1.

7. Three years after a Party establishes a numerical limit pursuant to paragraph 4, it shall consult with the other Party concerned with a view to determining a date after which the limit shall cease to apply.

ANNEX 1604.2
PROVISION OF INFORMATION

The obligations under Article 1604(2) shall take effect with respect to Mexico one year after the date of entry into force of this Agreement.

ANNEX 1608
COUNTRY-SPECIFIC DEFINITIONS

For purposes of this Chapter:

citizen means, with respect to Mexico, a national or a citizen according to the existing provisions of Articles 30 and 34, respectively, of the Mexican Constitution; and

existing means, as between:

(a) Canada and Mexico, and the United States and Mexico, in effect upon the date of entry into force of this Agreement; and

(b) Canada and the United States, in effect on January 1, 1989.

APPENDIX 1603.A
EXISTING IMMIGRATION MEASURES

1. In the case of Canada, the Immigration Act, R.S.C. 1985 c. I-2, as amended, and subsection 19(1) of the Immigration Regulations, 1978, as amended.

2. In the case of the United States, Section 101(a)(15)(B) of the Immigration and Nationality Act, 1952, as amended.

3. In the case of Mexico, Chapter III of the Ley General de Poblacion, 1974, as amended.

SCHEDULE I

Research and Design

• Technical, scientific, and statistical researchers conducting independent research, or research for an enterprise located in the territory of another Party.

Growth, Manufacture and Production

• Harvester owner supervising a harvesting crew admitted under applicable law.
• Purchasing and production management personnel conducting commercial transactions for an enterprise located in the territory of another Party.

Marketing

• Market researchers and analysts conducting independent research or analysis, or research or analysis for an enterprise located in the territory of another Party.
• Trade fair and promotional personnel attending a trade convention.

Sales

• Sales representatives and agents taking orders or negotiating contracts for goods or services for an enterprise located in the territory of another Party but not delivering goods or providing services.
Buyers purchasing for an enterprise located in the territory of another Party.

Distribution

• Transportation operators transporting goods or passengers to the territory of a Party from the territory of another Party or loading and transporting goods or passengers from the territory of a Party to the territory of another Party, with no loading and delivery within the territory of the Party into which entry is sought of goods located in or passengers boarding in the territory.
• With respect to temporary entry into the territory of the United States, Canadian customs brokers performing brokerage duties relating to the export of goods from the territory of the United States to or through the territory of Canada; with respect to temporary entry into the territory of Canada, United States customs brokers performing brokerage duties relating to the export of goods from the territory of Canada to or through the territory of the United States.
• Customs brokers consulting regarding the facilitation of the import or export of goods.

After-Sales Service

• Installers, repair and maintenance personnel, and supervisors, possessing specialized knowledge essential to a seller's contractual obligation, performing services or training workers to perform such services, pursuant to a warranty or other service contract incidental to the sale of commercial or industrial equipment or machinery, including computer software, purchased from an enterprise located outside the territory of the Party into which temporary entry is sought, during the life of the warranty or service agreement.

General Service

• Professionals engaging in a business activity at a professional level in a profession set out in Schedule II.

• Management and supervisory personnel engaging in a commercial transaction for an enterprise located in the territory of another Party.

• Financial services personnel (insurers, bankers or investment brokers) engaging in commercial transactions for an enterprise located in the territory of another Party.

• Public relations and advertising personnel consulting with business associates, and attending or participating in conventions.

• Tourism personnel (tour and travel agents, tour guides or tour operators) attending or participating in conventions or conducting a tour that has begun in the territory of another Party.

• Tour bus operators entering the territory of a Party:

(a) with a group of passengers on a bus tour that has begun in, and will return to, the territory of another Party.

(b) to meet a group of passengers on a bus tour that will end, and the predominant portion of which will take place, in the territory of another Party.

(c) with a group of passengers on a bus tour to be unloaded in the territory of the Party into which temporary entry is sought, and returning with no passengers or reloading with such group for transportation to the territory of another Party.

• Translators or interpreters performing services as employees of an enterprise located in the territory of another Party.

Definitions

For the purposes of this Schedule:

territory of another party means the territory of a Party other than the territory of the Party into which temporary entry is sought;

tour bus operator means a natural person, including relief personnel accompanying or following to join, necessary for the operation of a tour bus for the duration of a trip; and

transportation operator means a natural person, other than a tour bus operator, including relief personnel accompanying or following to join, necessary for the operation of a vehicle for the duration of a trip.

SCHEDULE II
PROFESSION[1]—MINIMUM EDUCATION REQUIREMENTS AND ALTERNATIVE CREDENTIALS

Accountant—Baccalaureate or Licenciatura Degree; or C.P.A., C.A., C.G.A., C.M.A.

Architect—Baccalaureate or Licenciatura Degree; or state/provincial license[2]

Computer Systems Analyst—Baccalaureate or Licenciatura Degree; or Post-Secondary Diploma[3] or Post-Secondary Certificate,[4] and three years experience

Disaster Relief Insurance Claims Adjuster (claims adjuster employed by an insurance company located in the territory of a Party, or an independent claims adjuster)—Baccalaureate or Licenciatura Degree, and successful completion of training in the appropriate areas of insurance adjustment pertaining to disaster relief claims; or three years of experience in claims adjustment, and successful completion of training in the appropriate areas of insurance adjustment pertaining to disaster relief claims

Economist—Baccalaureate or Licenciatura Degree

Engineer—Baccalaureate or Licenciatura Degree; or state/provincial license

Forester—Baccalaureate or Licenciatura Degree; or state/provincial license

Graphic Designer—Baccalaureate or Licenciatura Degree; or Post-Secondary Diploma or Post-Secondary Certificate, and three years experience

Hotel Manager—Baccalaureate or Licenciatura Degree in hotel/restaurant management; or Post-Secondary Diploma or Post-Secondary Certificate in hotel/restaurant management, and three years experience in hotel/restaurant management

Industrial Designer—Baccalaureate or Licenciatura Degree; or Post-Secondary Diploma or Post-Secondary Certificate, and three years experience

Interior Designer—Baccalaureate or Licenciatura Degree; or Post-Secondary Diploma or Post-Secondary Certificate, and three years experience

Land Surveyor—Baccalaureate or Licenciatura Degree; or state/provincial/federal license

Landscape Architect—Baccalaureate or Licenciatura Degree

Lawyer (including Notary in the Province of Quebec)—LL.B., J.D., LL.L., B.C.L., or Licenciatura Degree (five years); or membership in a state/provincial bar

Librarian—M.L.S. or B.L.S. (for which another Baccalaureate or Licenciatura Degree was a prerequisite)

Management Consultant—Baccalaureate or Licenciatura Degree; or equivalent professional experience as established by statement, or professional credential, attesting to five years experience as a management consultant, or five years experience in a field of specialty related to the consulting agreement

Mathematician (including Statistician)—Baccalaureate or Licenciatura Degree

Medical/Allied Professional

Dentist—D.D.S., D.M.D., Doctor en Odontologia, or Doctor en Cirugia Dental; or state/provincial license

Dietician—Baccalaureate or Licenciatura Degree; or state/provincial license

Medical Laboratory Technologist (Canada)/Medical Technologist (United States and Mexico)[5]—Baccalaureate or Licenciatura Degree; or Post-Secondary Diploma or Post-Secondary Certificate, and three years experience

Nutritionist—Baccalaureate or Licenciatura Degree

Occupational Therapist—Baccalaureate or Licenciatura Degree; or state/provincial license

Pharmacist—Baccalaureate or Licenciatura Degree; or state/provincial license

Physician (teaching and/or research only)—M.D. or Doctor en Medicina; or state/provincial license

Physiotherapist/Physical Therapist—Baccalaureate or Licenciatura Degree; or state/provincial license

Psychologist—State/provincial license or Licenciatura Degree

Recreational Therapist—Baccalaureate or Licenciatura Degree

Registered Nurse—State/provincial license or Licenciatura Degree

Veterinarian—D.V.M., D.M.V., or Doctor en Veterinaria; or state/provincial license

Range Manager/Range Conservationist—Baccalaureate or Licenciatura Degree

Research Assistant (Working in a post-secondary educational institution)—Baccalaureate or Licenciatura Degree

Scientific Technician/Technologist[6]—Possession of: (a) theoretical knowledge of any of the following disciplines: agricultural science, astronomy, biology, chemistry, engineering, forestry, geology, geophysics, meteorology, or physics; and (b) ability to solve practical problems in any of such disciplines, or the ability to apply principles of any of such disciplines to basic or applied research

Scientist

Agriculturist (including Agronomist)—Baccalaureate or Licenciatura Degree

Animal Breeder—Baccalaureate or Licenciatura Degree

Animal Scientist—Baccalaureate or Licenciatura Degree

Apiculturist—Baccalaureate or Licenciatura Degree

Astronomer—Baccalaureate or Licenciatura Degree

Biochemist—Baccalaureate or Licenciatura Degree

Biologist—Baccalaureate or Licenciatura Degree

Chemist—Baccalaureate or Licenciatura Degree

Dairy Scientist—Baccalaureate or Licenciatura Degree

Entomologist—Baccalaureate or Licenciatura Degree

Epidemiologist—Baccalaureate or Licenciatura Degree

Geneticist—Baccalaureate or Licenciatura Degree

Geologist—Baccalaureate or Licenciatura Degree

Geochemist—Baccalaureate or Licenciatura Degree

Geophysicist (including Oceanographer in Mexico and the United States)—Baccalaureate or Licenciatura Degree

Horticulturist—Baccalaureate or Licenciatura Degree

Meteorologist—Baccalaureate or Licenciatura Degree

Pharmacologist—Baccalaureate or Licenciatura Degree

Physicist (including Oceanographer in Canada)—Baccalaureate or Licenciatura Degree

Plant Breeder—Baccalaureate or Licenciatura Degree

Poultry Scientist—Baccalaureate or Licenciatura Degree

Soil Scientist—Baccalaureate or Licenciatura Degree

Zoologist—Baccalaureate or Licenciatura Degree

Social Worker—Baccalaureate or Licenciatura Degree

Sylviculturist (including Forestry Specialist)—Baccalaureate or Licenciatura Degree

Teacher

College—Baccalaureate or Licenciatura Degree

Seminary—Baccalaureate or Licenciatura Degree

University—Baccalaureate or Licenciatura Degree

Technical Publications Writer—Baccalaureate or Licenciatura Degree; or Post-Secondary Diploma or Post-Secondary Certificate, and three years experience

Urban Planner (including Geographer)—Baccalaureate or Licenciatura Degree

Vocational Counsellor—Baccalaureate or Licenciatura Degree

SCHEDULE III
UNITED STATES OF AMERICA

1. Commencing on the date of entry into force of this Agreement as between the United States and Mexico, the United States shall annually approve as many as 3,500 initial petitions of business persons of Mexico seeking temporary entry under Section D of Annex 1603 to engage in a business activity at a professional level in a profession set out in Schedule II.

2. For purposes of paragraph 1, the United States shall not take into account:

(a) the renewal of a period of temporary entry;

(b) the entry of a spouse or children accompanying or following to join the principal business person;

(c) an admission under Section 101(a)(15)(H)(i)(b) of Immigration and Nationality Act, 1952, as amended, including the worldwide numerical limit established by Section 214 (g)(1)(A) of such Act; or

(d) an admission under any other provision of Section 101(a)(15) of such Act relating to the entry of professionals.

3. Paragraphs 4 and 5 of Section D of Annex 1603 shall apply as between the United States and Mexico for no longer than:

(a) the period of such paragraphs or similar provisions may apply as between the United States and any other Party or non-Party; or

(b) 10 years after the date of entry into force of this Agreement as between such Parties, whichever period is shorter.

NOTES

1. A business person seeking temporary entry under this Schedule may also perform training functions relating to the profession, including conducting seminars.

2. The terms "state/provincial license" and "state/provincial/federal license" mean any document issued by a state, provincial or federal government, as the case may be, or under its authority, but not by a local government, that permits a person to engage in a regulated activity or profession.

3. The term "Post-Secondary Diploma" means a credential issued, upon completion of two or more years of post-secondary education, by an accredited academic institution in Canada or the United States.

4. The term "Post-Secondary Certificate" means a certificate issued, upon completion of two or more years of post-secondary education at an academic institution, by the federal government of Mexico or a state government in Mexico, an academic institution recognized by the federal government or a state government, or an academic institution created by federal or state law.

5. A business person in this category must be seeking temporary entry to perform in a laboratory chemical, biological, hematological, immunologic, microscopic or bacteriological tests, and analyses for diagnosis, treatment, or prevention of disease.

6. A business person in this category must be seeking temporary entry to work in direct support of professionals in agricultural sciences, astronomy, biology, chemistry, engineering, forestry, geology, geophysics, meteorology, or physics.

Appendix B

North American Free Trade Agreement Implementation Act

(Pub.L. 103-182, 107 Stat. 2057, December 8, 1993)

SUBTITLE D—Temporary Entry of Business Persons

Sec. 3412. Temporary Entry

(a) Nonimmigrant Traders and Investors.—Upon a basis of reciprocity secured by this Agreement, an alien who is a citizen of Canada or Mexico, and the spouse and children of any such alien if accompanying or following to join such alien, may, if otherwise eligible for a visa and if otherwise admissible into the United States under the Immigration and Nationality Act (8 U.S.C. 1011 et. seq.), be considered to be classifiable as a nonimmigrant under section 101(a)(15)(E) of such Act (8 U.S.C. 1011 (a)(15)(E)) if entering solely for a purpose specified in Section B of Annex 1603 of the Agreement, but only if any such purpose shall have been specified in such Annex on the date of entry into force of the Agreement. For purposes of this section, the term "citizen of Mexico" means "citizen" as defined in Annex 1608 of the Agreement.

(b) Nonimmigrant Professionals and Annual Numerical Limit. Section 214 of the Immigration and Nationality Act (8 U.S.C. 1084) is amended by redesignating subsection (e) as paragraph (1) of subsection (e) and adding after such paragraph (1), as redesignated, the following new paragraphs:

"(2) An alien who is a citizen of Canada or Mexico, and the spouse and children of any such alien if accompanying or following to join such alien, who seeks to enter the United States under and pursuant to the provisions of Section D of Annex 1603 of the North American Free Trade Agreement (in this subsection referred to as "NAFTA") to engage in business activities at a professional level as provided for in such Annex, may be admitted for such purpose under regulations of the Attorney General promulgated after consultation with the Secretaries of State and Labor. For purposes of this Act, including the issuance of entry documents and the application of subsection (b), such alien shall be treated as if seeking classification, or classifiable, as a nonimmigrant under section 101(a)(15). The admission of an alien who is a citizen of Mexico shall be subject to paragraphs (3), (4), and (5). For purposes of this paragraph and paragraphs (3), (4), and (5), the term "citizen of Mexico" means "citizen" as defined in Annex 1608 of NAFTA.

"(3) The Attorney General shall establish an annual numerical limit on admissions under paragraph (2) of aliens who are citizens of Mexico, as set forth in Appendix 1603.D.4 of Annex 1603 of NAFTA. Subject to paragraph (4), the annual numerical limit—

"(A) beginning with the second year that NAFTA is in force, may be increased in accordance with the provisions of paragraph 5(a) of Section D of such Annex, and

"(B) shall cease to apply as provided for in paragraph 3 of such Appendix.

"(4) The annual numerical limit referred to in paragraph (3) may be increased or shall cease to apply (other than by operation of paragraph 3 of such Appendix) only if—

"(A) the President has obtained advice regarding the proposed action from the appropriate advisory committees established under section 135 of the Trade Act of 1974 (19 U.S.C. 2155);

"(B) the President has submitted a report to the Committee on the Judiciary of the Senate and the Committee on the Judiciary of the House of Representatives that sets forth—

"(i) the action proposed to be taken and the reasons therefor, and

"(ii) the advice obtained under subparagraph (A);

"(C) a period of at least 60 calendar days that begins on the first day on which the President has met the requirements of subparagraphs (A) and (B) with respect to such action has expired; and

"(D) the President has consulted with such committees regarding the proposed action during the period referred to in subparagraph (C).

"(5) During the period that the provisions of Appendix 1603.D.4 of Annex 1603 of the NAFTA apply, the entry of an alien who is a citizen of Mexico under and pursuant to the provisions of Section D of Annex 1603 of NAFTA shall be subject to the attestation requirement of section 212(m), in the case of a registered nurse, or the application requirement of section 212(n), in the case of all other professions set out in Appendix 1603.D.1 of Annex 1603 of NAFTA, and the petition requirement of subsection (c), to the extent and in the manner prescribed in regulations promulgated by the Secretary of Labor, with respect to sections 212(m) and 212(n), and the Attorney General, with respect to subsection (c)."

(c) Labor disputes.—Section 214 of the Immigration and Nationality Act (8 U.S.C. 1184) is amended by adding at the end of the following new subsections:

"(j) Notwithstanding any other provisions of this Act, an alien who is a citizen of Canada or Mexico who seeks to enter the United States under and pursuant to the provisions of Section B, Section C, or Section D of Annex 1603 of the North American Free Trade Agreement, shall not be classified as a nonimmigrant under such provisions if there is in progress a strike or lockout in the course of a labor dispute in the occupational classification at the place or intended place of employment, unless such alien establishes, pursuant to regulations promulgated by the Attorney General, that the alien's entry will not affect adversely the settlement of the strike or lockout or the employment of any person who is involved in the strike or lockout. Notice of a determination under this subsection shall be given as may be required by paragraph 3 of article 1603 of such Agreement. For purposes of this subsection, the term 'citizen of Mexico' means 'citizen' as defined in Annex 1608 of such Agreement."

SEC. 342. EFFECTIVE DATE

The provisions of this subtitle take effect on the date the Agreement enters into force with respect to the United States [January 1, 1994].

Appendix C

Immigration and Naturalization Act

The INA was amended to include sections that covered the immigration provisions of NAFTA. Subsection (e) was added to the Act by s. 307(b) of the United States–Canada Free-Trade Agreement Implementation Act of 1988, Pub.L. 100–499, 102 Stat. 1877, Sept. 28. Subsection (e) was amended again, effective Jan. 1, 1994, by s. 341(b) of the NAFTA Implementation Act, Pub. L. 103–182, 107 Stat. 2057, Dec. 8, 1993. These sections of the INA are included to provide the exact wording since the text summarizes and paraphrases the meaning of the INA.

SEC. 214(e)

(1) Notwithstanding any other provision of this Act, an alien who is a citizen of Canada and seeks to enter the United States under and pursuant to the provisions of Annex 1502.1 (United States of America), Part C—Professionals, of the United States–Canada Free Trade Agreement to engage in business activities at a professional level as provided for therein may be admitted for such purpose under regulations of the Attorney General promulgated after consultation with the Secretaries of State and Labor.

(2) An alien who is a citizen of Canada or Mexico, and the spouse and children of any such alien if accompanying or following to join such alien, who seeks to enter the United States under and pursuant to the provisions of Section D of Annex 1603 of the North American Free Trade Agreement (in this subsection referred to as "NAFTA") to engage in business activities at a professional level as provided for in such Annex, may be admitted for such purpose under regulations of the Attorney General promulgated after consultation with the Secretaries of State and Labor. For purposes of this Act, including the issuance of entry documents and the application of subsection (b), such alien shall be treated as if seeking classification, or classifiable, as a nonimmigrant under section 101(a)(15). The admission of an alien who is a citizen of Mexico shall be subject to paragraphs (3), (4), and (5).

For purposes of this paragraph and paragraphs (3), (4), and (5), the term "citizen of Mexico" means "citizen" as defined in Annex 1608 of NAFTA.

(3) The Attorney General shall establish an annual numerical limit on admissions under paragraph (2) of aliens who are citizens of Mexico, as set forth in Appendix 1603.D.4 of Annex 1603 of the NAFTA. Subject to paragraph (4), the annual numerical limit—

(A) beginning with the second year that NAFTA is in force, may be increased in accordance with the provisions of paragraph 5(a) of Section D of such Annex, and

(B) shall cease to apply as provided for in paragraph 3 of such Appendix.

(4) The annual numerical limit referred to in paragraph (3) may be increased or shall cease to apply (other than by operation of paragraph 3 of such Appendix) only if—

(A) the President has obtained advice regarding the proposed action from the appropriate advisory committees established under section 135 of the Trade Act of 1974 (19 U.S.C. 2155);

(B) the President has submitted a report to the Committee on the Judiciary of the Senate and the Committee on the Judiciary of the House of Representatives that sets forth—

(i) the action proposed to be taken and the reasons therefor, and

(ii) the advice obtained under subparagraph (A);

(C) a period of at least 60 calendar days that begins on the first day on which the President has met the requirements of subparagraphs (A) and (B) with respect to such action has expired; and

(D) the President has consulted with such committees regarding the proposed action during the period referred to in subparagraph (C).

(5) During the period that the provisions of Appendix 1603.D.4 of Annex 1603 of NAFTA apply, the entry of an alien who is a citizen of Mexico under and pursuant to the provisions of Section D of Annex 1603 of NAFTA shall be subject to the attestation requirement of section 212(m), in the case of a registered nurse, or the application requirement of section 212(n), in the case of all other professions set out in Appendix 1603.D.1 of Annex 1603 of NAFTA, and the petition requirement of subsection (c), to the extent and in the manner prescribed in regulations promulgated by the Secretary of Labor, with respect to sections 212(m) and 212(n), and the Attorney General, with respect to subsection (c).

(j) Notwithstanding any other provision of this Act, an alien who is a citizen of Canada or Mexico who seeks to enter the United States under and pursuant to the provisions of Section B, Section C, or Section D of Annex 1603 of[the] North American Free Trade Agreement, shall not be classified as a nonimmigrant under such provisions if there is in progress a strike or lockout in the course of a labor dispute in the occupational classification at the place or intended place of employment, unless such alien establishes, pursuant to regulations promulgated by the Attorney General, that the alien's entry will not affect adversely the settlement of the strike or lockout or the employment of any person who is involved in the strike or lockout. Notice of a determination under this subsection shall be given as may be required by paragraph 3 of article 1603 of such Agreement. For purposes of this subsection, the term "citizen of Mexico" means "citizen" as defined in Annex 1608 of such Agreement.

Section 307, The United States–Canada Free-Trade Agreement Implementation Act of 1988

(Pub.L. 100-449, 102 Stat. 1876, September 28, 1988)

SEC. 307. TEMPORARY ENTRY FOR BUSINESS PERSONS

(a) Nonimmigrant Traders and Investors. Upon a basis of reciprocity secured by the United States–Canada Free Trade Agreement, a citizen of Canada, and the spouse and children of any such citizen if accompanying or following to join such citizen, may, if otherwise eligible for a visa and if otherwise admissible into the United States under the Immigration and Nationality Act (8 U.S.C. 1101 et. seq.), be considered to be classifiable as a nonimmigrant under section 101(a)(15)(E) of such Act (8 U.S.C. 1101 (a)(15)(E)) if entering solely for a purpose specified in Annex 1502.1 (United States of America), Part B—Traders and Investors, of such Agreement, but only if any such purpose shall have been specified in such Annex as of the date of entry into force of such Agreement.

(b) Nonimmigrant Professionals. Section 214 of the Immigration and Nationality Act (8 U.S.C. 1184) is amended by adding at the end thereof the following new subsection: "(e) Notwithstanding any other provision of this Act, an alien who is a citizen of Canada and seeks to enter the United States under and pursuant to the provisions of Annex 1502.1 (United States of America), Part C—Professionals, of the United States–Canada Free Trade Agreement to engage in business activities at a professional level as provided for therein may be admitted for such purpose under regulations of the Attorney General promulgated after consultation with the Secretaries of State and Labor."

Documents Recommended to Support a Petition for L-1 Intracompany Transferee

To assist in the preparation of the petition for an L-1 for an intracompany transferee, companies can use this checklist to ensure they have obtained all the supporting documentation to ensure a successful filing. The person responsible for preparing the petition should obtain originals or clear photocopies of all of the information listed. Mark off each item as it is collected. Using paper clips, not staples, to hold documents together will permit the easy photocopying of duplicate sets (one for the INS, one for the employee to take to the consulate in his or her home country, and for a file copy).

DOCUMENTS FOR FOREIGN CORPORATION

1. Documents to prove existence of foreign business
———(a) For a corporation, a certificate of incorporation, articles of incorporation, corporate by-laws, shareholders agreement, and other documents showing registration of corporation

For a partnership, partnership agreement and any other documents showing registration of partnership or partnership name

For a joint venture, joint venture agreement and any other documents showing registration of joint venture or joint venture name

For a sole proprietorship, documents showing date of start of business or registration of business name

———(b) description of ownership (e.g., list of shareholders, partners, etc.)
———(c) list of directors and officers, or principals who operate business activities
———(d) organizational chart (if it is a large company show the divisional and managerial subdivisions and include the titles of managers of each division, the title and name of the alien, the name of each division, and the number of employees in each division; if it is a smaller company show the structure

using the names and titles of individuals and the number of employees supervised by each executive or manager)

———(e) a chart showing how the U.S. business will fit into the foreign business organization

———(f) business cards of major executives

———(g) copy of annual report, showing company is still in existence

———(h) copy of yellow pages and white pages listing in local phone book

———(i) copy of business memberships in such groups as business organizations, chambers of commerce, and trade associations

———(j) copy of listing of business in directories

2. Documents to prove business operation of foreign corporation

———(a) profit and loss statement

———(b) balance sheet

———(c) tax return

———(d) list of major customers

———(e) list of major suppliers

———(f) copies of brochures outlining products or services

———(g) copies of advertisements in newspapers for products or services

———(h) description of business operation, or business plan

———(i) list of sales or service business offices or locations

———(j) copy of all relevant business permits, licenses, or registrations

———(k) copy of documents for rented business premise (e.g., lease and rent receipts); documents for business owned property (e.g., deeds and mortgages)

———(l) samples of business invoices and contracts that do not disclose business secrets (as many as possible to show international as well as national sales of goods or services) and supplier contracts

———(m) copies from magazines and newspapers of articles about business or major executives, quoting major executives, new product notices, key personnel notices of key personnel promotions or awards

———(n) annual reports

3. Documents to prove alien was employed as a Multinational Executive or Manager or person with specialized knowledge for one of the last three years by a foreign corporation outside the United States

———(a) job title

———(b) detailed job description showing alien as executive or manager

———(c) alien employee payroll records

———(d) business card of alien in foreign business position

———(e) organizational chart showing alien's position

———(f) copies of brochures, annual reports, or other corporate documents showing alien's name and position

———(g) copy of such documents as the employment contract and pay stubs

———(h) alien's personal income tax returns

DOCUMENTS FOR U.S. BUSINESS

1A. If business is to be developed

———(a) comprehensive business plan (include sections on the legal structure of business, potential customers and suppliers, competition, facilities and equipment needed, staff, products or services business will sell, projected time-line for start-up, marketing and advertising plan, and a three-year cash flow projection, income statement, and balance sheet

———(b) details of the L-1 executive's role in creating the new business

———(c) lease for business premises

1B. If U.S. business is already in existence

———(a) certificate of incorporation, partnership agreement, joint venture agreement showing U.S. business is an affiliate in one of the following ways:

      (i) one of two subsidiaries both owned by same parent or individual

      (ii) one of two legal entities entirely owned and controlled by the same group of individuals, each owning the same share in each entity

      (iii) U.S. accounting or consulting service, owned by foreign accounting or consulting service

———(b) list of directors, officers, and shareholders

———(c) organizational chart showing L-1 employee (if it is a large company, show the divisional and managerial subdivisions and include the titles of managers of each division, the title and name of the alien, the name of each division, and the number of employees in each division; if it is a smaller company, show the structure using the names and titles of individuals and the number of employees supervised by each)

———(d) business cards of major executives

———(e) copy of annual report

———(f) copy of yellow pages listing

———(g) copy of business memberships in such groups as business organizations, chambers of commerce, and trade associations

———(h) copy of listings of business in directories for industry

———(i) income tax returns

———(j) profit and loss statement, showing company has income to pay executive wages

———(k) balance sheet, showing company can pay executive wages

———(l) list of major customers

———(m) list of major suppliers

———(n) copies of brochures outlining products or services

———(o) copies of advertisements in newspapers for products or services

———(p) description of business operation or business plan

———(q) list of sales or service business offices or locations

———(r) copy of all relevant business permits, licenses, or registrations

———(s) copy of documents for rented business premise (e.g., lease and rent receipts); documents for business owned property (e.g., deeds and mortgages)

———(t) samples of business invoices and contracts that do not disclose business secrets (as many as possible to show international as well as national sales of goods or services) and supplier contracts

———(u) copies from magazines and newspapers of articles about business or major executives, including statements of major executives, new product notices, and notices of key personnel promotions or awards

2. Documents to prove the alien will be employed as a Multinational Executive or Manager for the U.S. business

————(a) job title

————(b) detailed job description

————(c) letter from the U.S. business offering employment as executive or manager, setting out the title, job description, and salary (in executive level salary range)

————(d) business card (if any)

————(e) organizational chart showing alien's position

————(f) copy of employment contract (if any)

————(g) copy of alien's resume

————(h) copy of alien's academic degrees and transcripts

————(i) copies of all awards, recognitions, and special achievements regarding employment

————(j) copies of all articles written by or about alien related to employment in foreign corporation

Appendix F

List of INS Service Center Addresses

All TN applications and extensions must be filed at the Northern Service Center, regardless of where the place of work is located. Other filings, such as extensions for spouses and for B visas, L visas, and E visas should be filed at the service center having jurisdiction over the location of the workplace.

INS Headquarters
425 Eye Street, N.W.
Washington, DC 20536

INS Service Center, Vermont (Eastern)
P.O. Box 9589
St. Albans, VT 05479–9589

INS Service Center, Nebraska (Northern)
850 "S" Street
Lincoln, NE 68501

INS Service Center, Texas (Southern)
The following are addresses to file forms with the Texas Service Center:

I-485
USINS TSC
P.O. Box 851804
Mesquite, TX 75185–1804

I-129
USINS TSC
P.O. Box 852211
Mesquite, TX 75185–2211

I-765
USINS TSC
P.O. Box 851041
Mesquite, TX 75185–1041

I-539
LEGALIZATION
USINS TSC
P.O. Box 851182
Mesquite, TX 75185–1182

CORRESPONDENCE
USINS TSC
P.O. Box 851488
Mesquite, TX 75185–1488

ADMINISTRATION
USINS TSC
P.O. Box 852005
Mesquite, TX 75185–2005

INS Service Center, California (Western)
P.O. Box 10589
Laguna Niguel, CA 92607–0589

Appendix G

Translation of Documents into English

All documents submitted to the INS in support of any application or petition must be in the English language or include an English language translation. Documents can be translated by anyone who is capable of translating a foreign language document into English and need not be translated by a professional translator. The translator must produce a typewritten translation and include a certification that the translation is accurate. An example of a certification is:

> I (their name), an individual, certify that I am competent to translate (name of language) to English, and certify that the translation is an accurate English translation of (name of document, e.g., birth certificate), a (name of language) document.
> Signature

The translation should be stapled to a photocopy of the document. The translator should put his or her signature on the photocopy of the document as well as below the above statement, which is typed below the translation.

Appendix H

Credential Evaluation

If a citizen of Canada or Mexico is obtaining a TN or other status under NAFTA, the employer should obtain a credential evaluation to show that the degree held by the TN professional meets the requirements and the regulations of NAFTA. Below is a list of companies that provide credential evaluations for immigration and other purposes. This list does not contain all organizations that provide this service. The authors are providing this list as an assistance to readers and are not making any representations or warranties about the services any or all of the businesses may provide. The authors have no relationship with, or interest in, any of the credential evaluation businesses listed here.

International Education Research Foundation, Inc.
P.O. Box 6694
Los Angeles, CA 90066
Phone: 310–390–6276, ext. 143
Fax: 310–397–7686
e-mail: jschuning@ierf.org

International Consultants of Delaware, Inc.
109 Barksdale Professional Center
Newark, DE 19711–3258
Phone: 302–737–8715
Fax: 302–737–8756
e-mail: icd@icdel.com

Educational Assessment & Evaluation, Inc.
1884 Barber Creek Road
Statham, GA 30666
Phone/Fax: 770–725–1753
e-mail: edassess@aol.com

Global Education Group, Inc.
407 Lincoln Road, Suite 2H
Miami Beach, FL 33139
Phone: 305–534–8745
Fax: 305–534–3487
e-mail: globaled@icanect.net
web site: www.globaledu.com

Academic Credentials Evaluation Institute, Inc.
P.O. Box 6908
Beverly Hills, CA 90212
Phone: 310–275–3530
Fax: 310–275–3428

World Education Services, Inc.
P.O. Box 745
Old Chelsea Station
New York, NY 10113–0745
Phone: 212–966–6311
Fax: 212–966–6395

The Knowledge Company
10201 Democracy Lane, Suite 403,
Fairfax, VA 22030–2321
Phone: 703–359–3520
Fax: 703–359–3523
e-mail: tkco@knowledgecompany.com
web site: http://www.knowledgecompany.com

Appendix I

Information Required by the Employer to Complete INS Form I-129

To complete the INS form I-129, an employer will need to include some standard information. All of the following information will be required to complete the form I-129, since an incomplete form will result in a rejection of the petition. In addition to the information to complete the form, employers should obtain photocopies of the employee's passport, both sides of the I-94 (if any), degrees and transcripts, any valid licenses for the profession or occupation, and the resume. If the employee had an E, L-1, or TN status with a different employer, the new employer should obtain a photocopy of all completed form I-129s that were previously filed, all approval notices, and any other documents associated with the previous filings, approvals, or rejections, and exact dates of employment in a nonimmigrant status including start and ending dates.

An employer should make an information sheet to include in the employee's file so this information is readily available when an extension is desired.

Information that is required includes:

Information about the employer company

Company or organization name

Complete street address

IRS Tax Number

Type of business

Year business was established

Number of employees (current details at time form is filed)

Gross annual income (current details at time form is filed)

Net annual income (current details at time form is filed)

Information about the NAFTA Employee

Full name (from passport)

Date of birth

Country of birth (if not Canada or Mexico, obtain a photocopy of naturalization certificate to show employee is a citizen of Canada or Mexico)

Social Security number (if any)

A# (if any)

Date of Arrival in the United States (if the employee is currently in the United States)

Current I-94 number (if the employee is currently in the United States. Retain a photocopy of both sides of this form)

Current nonimmigrant status (if employee is currently in the United States)

Date I-94 expires (if any)

Consulate outside the United States to notify, if required (this must be included even if employee is currently in the United States)

Employee's foreign address

Valid passport (photocopy)

Spouse and children who will accompany employee (name, date, and country of birth, relationship to employee, and foreign address for each)

The employee's status in the category being petitioned for (start and ending dates in the category in last seven years, employer name and address)

Details on any denial of this category by INS for the employee for the last seven years

Information about the job

Job title

Nontechnical description of the job

Address where the employee will work

Full-time or part-time with hours per week

Wages per week or per year

Other compensation (how derived and amount)

Dates of extended employment, start and ending date

Appendix J

INS Forms

INS forms may be obtained from local INS offices and Service Centers. They may also be created in immigration software programs. These are the forms that will be required for citizens of Canada or Mexico entering under NAFTA:

Form I-129

Form I-129 Supplement E/L E Classification

Form I-129 Supplement E/L L Classification

Form I-539

ETA 9035

Form I-9

U.S. Department of Justice
Immigration and Naturalization Service

For sale by the Superintendent of Documents
U.S. Government Printing Office
Washington, DC 20402

OMB #1115-0168

Petition for a Nonimmigrant Worker

START HERE - Please Type or Print

Part 1. Information about the employer filing this petition.
If the employer is an individual, use the top name line. Organizations should use the second line.

Family Name	Given Name	Middle Initial

Company or Organization Name

Address - Attn:

Street Number and Name		Apt. #
City	State or Province	
Country	ZIP/Postal Code	

IRS Tax #

Part 2. Information about this Petition.
(See instructions to determine the fee).

1. **Requested Nonimmigrant Classification:**
   (write classification symbol at right) _____

2. **Basis for Classification** (check one)
   a. ☐ New employment
   b. ☐ Continuation of previously approved employment without change
   c. ☐ Change in previously approved employment
   d. ☐ New concurrent employment

3. **Prior petition.** If you checked other than "New Employment" in item 2. (above) give the most recent prior petition number for the worker(s):

4. **Requested Action:** (check one)
   a. ☐ Notify the office in Part 4 so the person(s) can obtain a visa or be admitted (NOTE: a petition is not required for an E-1, E-2, or R visa).
   b. ☐ Change the person(s) status and extend their stay since they are all now in the U.S. in another status (see instructions for limitations). This is available only where you check "New Employment" in item 2, above.
   c. ☐ Extend or amend the stay of the person(s) since they now hold this status.

5. **Total number of workers in petition:**

   (See instructions for where more than one worker can be included.)

Part 3. Information about the person(s) you are filing for.
Complete the blocks below. Use the continuation sheet to name each person included in this petition.

If an entertainment group, give their group name.

Family Name	Given Name	Middle Initial
Date of Birth (Month/Day/Year)	Country of Birth	
Social Security #	A #	

If in the United States, complete the following:

Date of Arrival (Month/Day/Year)	I-94 #
Current Nonimmigrant Status	Expires (Month/Day/Year)

Form I-129 (Rev. 12/11/91) N   *Continued on back.*

FOR INS USE ONLY

Returned	Receipt

Resubmitted

Reloc Sent

Reloc Rec'd

Interviewed
☐ Petitioner
☐ Beneficiary

Class: _____
# of Workers: _____
Priority Number: _____
Validity Dates: From _____
To _____

☐ **Classification Approved**
☐ Consulate/POE/PFI Notified

At: _____
☐ Extension Granted
☐ COS/Extension Granted

Partial Approval (explain)

Action Block

To Be Completed by
Attorney or Representative, if any
☐ Fill in box if G-28 is attached to represent the applicant

VOLAG#

ATTY State License #

Part 4. Processing Information.

a. If the person named in Part 3 is outside the U.S. or a requested extension of stay or change of status cannot be granted, give the U.S. consulate or inspection facility you want notified if this petition is approved.

Type of Office (check one): ☐ Consulate	☐ Pre-flight inspection	☐ Port of Entry
Office Address (City)		U.S. State or Foreign Country
Person's Foreign Address		

b. Does each person in this petition have a valid passport?
  ☐ Not required to have passport   ☐ No - explain on separate paper ☐ Yes

c. Are you filing any other petitions with this one?   ☐ No   ☐ Yes - How many? _____
d. Are applications for replacement/Initial I-94's being filed with this petition?   ☐ No   ☐ Yes - How many? _____
e. Are applications by dependents being filed with this petition?   ☐ No   ☐ Yes - How many? _____
f. Is any person in this petition in exclusion or deportation proceedings?   ☐ No   ☐ Yes - explain on separate paper
g. Have you ever filed an immigrant petition for any person in this petition?   ☐ No   ☐ Yes - explain on separate paper
h. If you indicated you were filing a new petition in Part 2, within the past 7 years has any person in this petition:

  1) ever been given the classification you are now requesting?   ☐ No   ☐ Yes - explain on separate paper
  2) ever been denied the classification you are now requesting?   ☐ No   ☐ Yes - explain on separate paper

i. If you are filing for an entertainment group, has any person in this petition not been with the group for at least 1 year?
  ☐ No   ☐ Yes - explain on separate paper

Part 5. Basic Information about the proposed employment and employer.
Attach the supplement relating to the classification you are requesting.

Job Title	Nontechnical Description of Job
Address where the person(s) will work if different from the address in Part 1.	

Is this a full-time position?		Wages per week
☐ No - Hours per week	☐ Yes	or per year

Other Compensation (Explain)	Value per week or per year	Dates of Intended employment From: To:
Type of Petitioner - check one: ☐ U.S. citizen or permanent resident	☐ Organization	☐ Other - explain on separate paper
Type of business:		Year established:
Current Number of Employees	Gross Annual Income	Net Annual Income

Part 6. Signature.
Read the information on penalties in the instructions before completing this section.

I certify, under penalty of perjury under the laws of the United States of America, that this petition, and the evidence submitted with it, is all true and correct. If filing this on behalf of an organization, I certify that I am empowered to do so by that organization. If this petition is to extend a prior petition, I certify that the proposed employment is under the same terms and conditions as in the prior approved petition. I authorize the release of any information from my records, or from the petitioning organization's records, which the Immigration and Naturalization Service needs to determine eligibility for the benefit being sought.

Signature and title	Print Name	Date

Please Note: If you do not completely fill out this form and the required supplement, or fail to submit required documents listed in the instructions, then the person(s) filed for may not be found eligible for the requested benefit, and this petition may be denied.

Part 7. Signature of person preparing form if other than above.

I declare that I prepared this petition at the request of the above person and it is based on all information of which I have any knowledge.

Signature	Print Name	Date
Firm Name and Address		

OMB #1115-0168

U.S. Department of Justice
Immigration and Naturalization Service

E Classification
Supplement to Form I-129

Name of person or organization filing petition:

Name of person you are filing for:

Classification sought (check one):
☐ E-1 Treaty trader ☐ E-2 Treaty investor

Name of country signatory to treaty with U.S.

Section 1. **Information about the Employer Outside the U.S. (if any)**

Name	Address

Alien's Position - Title, duties and number of years employed | Principal Product, merchandise or service

Total Number of Employees

Section 2. **Additional Information about the U.S. Employer.**

The U.S. company is, to the company outside the U.S. (check one):
☐ Parent ☐ Branch ☐ Subsidiary ☐ Affiliate ☐ Joint Venture

Date and Place of Incorporation or establishment in the U.S.

Nationality of Ownership (Individual or Corporate)

Name	Nationality	Immigration Status	% Ownership

Assets	Net Worth	Total Annual Income

Staff in the U.S.	Executive/Manager	Specialized Qualifications or Knowledge
Nationals of Treaty Country in E or L Status		
Total number of employees in the U.S.		

Total number of employees the alien would supervise; or describe the nature of the specialized skills essential to the U.S. company.

Section 3. **Complete if filing for an E-1 Treaty Trader**

Total Annual Gross Trade/Business of the U.S. company   For Year Ending

$

Percent of total gross trade which is between the U.S. and the country of which the treaty trader organization is a national.

Section 4. **Complete if filing for an E-2 Treaty Investor**

Total Investment:	Cash	Equipment	Other
	$	$	$
	Inventory	Premises	Total
	$	$	$

Form I-129 Supplement E/L (12/11/91) N

OMB #1115-0168

U.S. Department of Justice
Immigration and Naturalization Service

L Classification
Supplement to Form I-129

Name of person or organization filing petition:

Name of person you are filing for:

This petition is (check one): ☐ An individual petition   ☐ A blanket petition

Section 1.   Complete this section if filing an individual petition.

Classification sought (check one): ☐ L-1A manager or executive   ☐ L-1B specialized knowledge

List the alien's, and any dependent family members' prior periods of stay in an L classification in the U.S. for the last seven years. Be sure to list only those periods in which the alien and/or family members were actually in the U.S. in an L classification.

Name and address of employer abroad

Dates of alien's employment with this employer. Explain any interruptions in employment.

Description of the alien's duties for the past 3 years.

Description of alien's proposed duties in the U.S.

Summarize the alien's education and work experience.

The U.S. company is, to the company abroad: (check one)
☐ Parent   ☐ Branch   ☐ Subsidiary   ☐ Affiliate   ☐ Joint Venture

Describe the stock ownership and managerial control of each company.

Do the companies currently have the same qualifying relationship as they did during the one-year period of the alien's employment with the company abroad?   ☐ Yes   ☐ No (attach explanation)

Is the alien coming to the U.S. to open a new office?
☐ Yes (explain in detail on separate paper)   ☐ No

Section 2.   Complete this section if filing a Blanket Petition.

List all U.S. and foreign parent, branches, subsidiaries and affiliates included in this petition. (Attach a separate paper if additional space is needed.)

Name and Address   Relationship

Explain in detail on separate paper.

Form I-129 Supplement E/L (12/11/91) N

START HERE - Please Type or Print

FOR INS USE ONLY

Part 1.   Information about you.

Family Name	Given Name	Middle Initial

Address - In Care of:

Street # and Name		Apt. #

City	State

Zip Code

Date of Birth (month/day/year)	Country of Birth

Social Security # (if any)	A# (if any)

Date of Last Arrival Into the U.S.	I-94#

Current Nonimmigrant Status	Expires on (month/day/year)

Returned	Receipt
Date _____	
Resubmitted	
Date _____	
Reloc Sent	
Date _____	
Reloc Rec'd	
Date _____	
Date _____	
☐ Applicant Interviewed	

Part 2.   Application Type.   (See instructions for fee.)

1. **I am applying for:** (check one)
   a. ☐ an extension of stay in my current status
   b. ☐ a change of status. The new status I am requesting is: _____
2. **Number of people included in this application:** (check one)
   a. ☐ I am the only applicant
   b. ☐ Members of my family are filing this application with me.
      The Total number of people included in this application is _____
      (complete the supplement for each co-applicant)

☐ *Extension Granted*
   to (date):_____

☐ *Change of Status/Extension Granted*
New Class:_____   To (date):_____

If denied:
☐ Still within period of stay

☐ V/D to: _____

☐ S/D to:_____

☐ Place under docket control

Part 3.   Processing information.

1. I/We request that my/our current or requested status be extended until (month/day/year) _____
2. Is this application based on an extension or change of status already granted to your spouse, child or parent?
   ☐ No   ☐ Yes (receipt # _____)
3. Is this application being filed based on a separate petition or application to give your spouse, child or parent an extension or change of status?
   ☐ No   ☐ Yes, filed with this application   ☐ Yes, filed previously and pending with INS
4. If you answered yes to question 3, give the petitioner or applicant name:

   If the application is pending with INS, also give the following information.

   Office filed at_____   Filed on_____   (date)

Remarks

Action Block

Part 4.   Additional information.

1. For applicant #1, provide passport information:

Country of issuance	Valid to: (month/day/year)

2. Foreign address:

Street # and Name		Apt#

City or Town	State or Province

Country	Zip or Postal Code

To Be Completed by
Attorney or *Representative*, if any
☐ Fill in box if G-28 is attached to represent the applicant

VOLAG#

ATTY State License #

Form I-539 (Rev. 12-2-91)   **Continued on back.**

Part 4. Additional Information. *(continued)*

3. Answer the following questions. If you answer yes to any question, explain on separate paper.	Yes	No
a. Are you, or any other person included in this application, an applicant for an immigrant visa or adjustment of status to permanent residence?		
b. Has an immigrant petition ever been filed for you, or for any other person included in this application?		
c. Have you, or any other person included in this application ever been arrested or convicted of any criminal offense since last entering the U.S.?		
d. Have you, or any other person included in this application done anything which violated the terms of the nonimmigrant status you now hold?		
e. Are you, or any other person included in this application, now in exclusion or deportation proceedings?		
f. Have you, or any other person included in this application, been employed in the U.S. since last admitted or granted an extension or change of status?		

If you answered YES to question 3f, give the following information on a separate paper: Name of person, name of employer, address of employer, weekly income, and whether specifically authorized by INS.

If you answered NO to question 3f, fully describe how you are supporting yourself on a separate paper. Include the source and the amount and basis for any income.

Part 5. Signature. *Read the information on penalties in the instructions before completing this section. You must file this application while in the United States.*

I certify under penalty of perjury under the laws of the United States of America that this application, and the evidence submitted with it, is all true and correct. I authorize the release of any information from my records which the Immigration and Naturalization Service needs to determine eligibility for the benefit I am seeking.

Signature	Print your name	Date

Please Note: *If you do not completely fill out this form, or fail to submit required documents listed in the instructions, you cannot be found eligible for the requested document and this application will have to be denied.*

Part 6. Signature of person preparing form if other than above. *(Sign below)*

I declare that I prepared this application at the request of the above person and it is based on all information of which I have knowledge.

Signature	Print Your Name	Date

Firm Name
and Address

(Please remember to enclose the mailing label with your application)

Labor Condition Application for H-1B Nonimmigrants	U.S. Department of Labor Employment and Training Administration U.S. Employment Service	

1. Full Legal Name of Employer	5. Employer's Address (No., Street, City, State, and ZIP Code)	OMB Approval No.: 1205-0310 Expiration Date: 11-30-97
2. Federal Employer I.D. Number		
3. Employer's Telephone No. (　　　)	6. Address Where Documentation is Kept (If different than item 5)	
4. Employer's FAX No. (　　　)		

7. OCCUPATIONAL INFORMATION (Use attachment if additional space is needed)

(a) Three-digit Occupational Group Code (From Appendix 2): _____　(b) Job Title (Check Box if Part-Time): _____ ☐

(c) No. of H-1B Nonimmigrants	(d) Rate of Pay	(e) Prevailing Wage Rate and its Source (see instructions)	(f) Period of Employment From　To	(g) Location(s) Where H-1B Nonimmigrants Will Work (see instructions)
_____	$_____	$_____ ☐SESA ☐Other:_____	_____ _____	_____
_____	$_____	$_____ ☐SESA ☐Other:_____	_____ _____	_____

8. EMPLOYER LABOR CONDITION STATEMENTS (Employers are required to develop and maintain documentation supporting labor condition statements 8(a) and 8(d). Employers are further required to make available for public examination a copy of the labor condition application and necessary supporting documentation within one (1) working day after the date on which the application is filed with DOL. Check **each** box to indicate that the employer will comply with **each** statement.)

☐ (a)　H-1B nonimmigrants will be paid at least the actual wage level paid by the employer to all other individuals with similar experience and qualifications for the specific employment in question or the prevailing wage level for the occupation in the area of employment, whichever is higher.

☐ (b)　The employment of H-1B nonimmigrants will not adversely affect the working conditions of workers similarly employed in the area of intended employment.

☐ (c)　On the date this application is signed and submitted, there is not a strike, lockout or work stoppage in the course of a labor dispute in the occupation in which H-1B nonimmigrants will be employed at the place of employment. If such a strike or lockout occurs after this application is submitted, I will notify ETA within 3 days of the occurrence of such a strike or lockout and the application will not be used in support of petition filings with INS for H-1B nonimmigrants to work in the same occupation at the place of employment until ETA determines the strike or lockout has ceased.

☐ (d)　A copy of this application has been, or will be, provided to each H-1B nonimmigrant employed pursuant to this application, and, as of this date, notice of this application has been provided to workers employed in the occupation in which H-1B nonimmigrants will be employed: (check appropriate box)

　　☐ (i)　Notice of this filing has been provided to the bargaining representative of workers in the occupation in which H-1B nonimmigrants will be employed; or

　　☐ (ii)　There is no such bargaining representative; therefore, a notice of this filing has been posted and was, or will remain, posted for 10 days in at least two conspicuous locations where H-1B nonimmigrants will be employed.

9. DECLARATION OF EMPLOYER. Pursuant to 28 U.S.C. 1746, I declare under penalty of perjury that the information provided on this form is true and correct. In addition, I declare that I will comply with the Department of Labor regulations governing this program and, in particular, that I will make this application, supporting documentation, and other records, files and documents available to officials of the Department of Labor, upon such official's request, during any investigation under this application or the Immigration and Nationality Act.

Name and Title of Hiring or Other Designated Official	Signature	Date

Complaints alleging misrepresentation of material facts in the labor condition application and/or failure to comply with the terms of the labor condition application may be filed with any office of the Wage and Hour Division of the United States Department of Labor.

AN APPLICATION CERTIFIED BY DOL MUST BE FILED IN SUPPORT OF AN H-1B VISA PETITION WITH THE INS.

FOR U.S. GOVERNMENT AGENCY USE ONLY: By virtue of my signature below, I acknowledge that this application is hereby certified and will be valid from _____ through _____.

Signature and Title of Authorized DOL Official	ETA Case No.	Date

Subsequent DOL Action:　Suspended _____ (date) Invalidated _____ (date) Withdrawn _____ (date)

The Department of Labor is not the guarantor of the accuracy, truthfulness or adequacy of a certified labor condition application.

Public reporting burden for this collection of information is estimated to average 1½ hour per response, including the time for reviewing instructions searching existing data sources, gathering and maintaining the data needed, and completing and reviewing the collection of information. Send comments regarding this burden estimate or any other aspect of this collection of information, including suggestions for reducing this burden, to the Office of U.S. Employment Service, Department of Labor, Room N-4470 and/or the Office of IRM Policy, DOL, Room N-1301, 200 Constitution Avenue, N.W., Washington, DC 20210. (1205-0310).

DO NOT SEND THE COMPLETED FORM TO EITHER OF THESE OFFICES　　　　ETA 9035 (Rev. Dec. 1994)

Appendix 2 (Not To Be Codified in the CFR): DOT Three-Digit Occupational Groups Codes for Professional, Technical and Managerial Occupations and Fashion Models

Printed below is a copy of DOT Three-Digit Occupational Groups Codes for Professional, Technical and Managerial Occupations and Fashion Models.

Three-Digit Occupational Groups

Professional, Technical, and Managerial Occupations and Fashion Models

Occupations in Architecture, Engineering, and Surveying

001   Architectural Occupations
002   Aeronautical engineering Occupations
003   Electrical/Electronics Engineering Occupations
005   Civil Engineering Occupations
006   Ceramic Engineering Occupations
007   Mechanical Engineering Occupations
008   Chemical Engineering Occupations
010   Mining and Petroleum Engineering Occupations
011   Metallurgy and Metallurgical Engineering Occupations
012   Industrial Engineering Occupations
013   Agricultural Engineering Occupations
014   Marine Engineering Occupations
015   Nuclear Engineering Occupations
017   Drafters
018   Surveying/Cartographic Occupations
019   Other Occupations in Architecture, Engineering, and Surveying

Occupations in Mathematics and Physical Sciences

020   Occupations in Mathematics
021   Occupations in Astronomy
022   Occupations in Chemistry
023   Occupations in Physics
024   Occupations in Geology
025   Occupations in Meteorology
029   Other Occupations in Mathematics and Physical Sciences

Computer-Related Occupations

030   Occupations in Systems Analysis and Programming
031   Occupations in Data Communications and Networks
032   Occupations in Computer System User Support
033   Occupations in Computer System Technical Support
039   Other Computer-Related Occupations

Occupations in Life Sciences

040   Occupations in Agricultural Sciences
041   Occupations in Biological Sciences
045   Occupations in Psychology
049   Other Occupations in Life Sciences

Occupations in Social Sciences

050   Occupations in Economics
051   Occupations in Political Science
052   Occupations in History
054   Occupations in Sociology
055   Occupations in Anthropology
059   Other Occupations in Social Sciences

Occupations in Medicine and Health

070   Physicians and Surgeons
071   Osteopaths
072   Dentists
073   Veterinarians
074   Pharmacists
076   Therapists
077   Dieticians
078   Occupations in Medical and Dental Technology
079   Other Occupations in Medicine and Health

Occupations in Education

090   Occupations in College and University Education
091   Occupations in Secondary School Education
092   Occupations in Preschool, Primary School, and Kindergarten Education
094   Occupations in Education of Persons With Disabilities
096   Home Economists and Farm Advisers
097   Occupations in Vocational Education
099   Other Occupations in Education

Occupations in Museum, Library, and Archival Sciences

100   Librarians
101   Archivists
102   Museum Curators and Related Occupations
109   Other Occupations in Museum, Library, and Archival Sciences

Occupations in Law and Jurisprudence

110   Lawyers
111   Judges
119   Other Occupations in Law and Jurisprudence

Occupations in Religion and Theology

120   Clergy
129   Other Occupations in Religion and Theology

Occupations in Writing

131   Writers
132   Editors: Publication, Broadcast, and Script
139   Other Occupations in Writing

Occupations in Art

141   Commercial Artists: Designers and Illustrators, Graphic Arts
142   Environmental, Product, and Related Designers
149   Other Occupations in Art

Occupations in Entertainment and Recreation

152   Occupations in Music
159   Other Occupations in Entertainment and Recreation

Occupations in Administrative Specializations

160   Accountants, Auditors, and Related Occupations
161   Budget and Management Systems Analysis Occupations
162   Purchasing Management Occupations
163   Sales and Distribution Management Occupations
164   Advertising Management Occupations
165   Public Relations Management Occupations
166   Personnel Administration Occupations
168   Inspectors and Investigators, Managerial and Public Service
169   Other Occupations in Administrative Occupations

Managers and Officials

180   Agriculture, Forestry and Fishing Industry Managers and Officials
181   Mining Industry Managers and Officials
182   Construction Industry Managers and Officials
183   Manufacturing Industry Managers and Officials
184   Transportation, Communication, and Utilities Industry Managers and Officials
185   Wholesale and Retail Trade Managers and Officials
186   Finance, Insurance, and Real Estate Managers and Officials
187   Service Industry Managers and Officials
188   Public Administration Managers and Officials
189   Miscellaneous Managers and Officials

Miscellaneous Professional, Technical, and Managerial Occupations

195   Occupations in Social and Welfare Work
199   Miscellaneous Professional, Technical, and Managerial Occupations

Sales Promotion Occupations

297   Fashion Models

[FR Doc. 95–1394 Filed 1–18–95; 8:45 am]
BILLING CODE 4510–30–M

Three-Digit Occupational Groups Codes
Professional, Technical and Managerial Occupations
and Fashion Models

The following occupational groups and corresponding codes do not appear in the appendix to the interim final rule. I assume they also are not contained in the computer tracking system.

017　Drafters, Not Elsewhere Classified (NEC)
018　Surveying/Cartographic Occupations
052　Occupations in History[1]
075　Registered Nurses
137　Interpreters and Translators
141　Commercial Artist: Designers and Illustrators, Graphic Arts
143　Occupations in Photography
144　Fine Artist: Painters, Sculptors, and Related Occupations
150　Occupations in Dramatics
151　Occupations in Dancing
153　Occupations in Athletics and Sports
162　Purchasing Management Occupations
163　Sales and Distribution Management Occupations
166　Personnel Administration Occupations[2]
168　Inspectors and Investigators, Managerial and Public Service
191　Agents and Appraisers, NEC
193　Radio Operators
194　Sound, Film, and Videotape Recording, and Reproduction Occupations
196　Airplane Pilots and Navigators
197　Ship Captains, Mates, Pilots, and Engineers
198　Railroad Conductors

---

[1] Note that "Occupations in Sociology," which did appear in the appendix, was erroneously classified as "052" and should have been "054." The "052" code actually pertains to the "Occupations in History" group.

[2] Erroneously classified as "168 Personnel Management Occupations" in appendix.

U.S. Department of Justice
Immigration and Naturalization Service

OMB No. 1115-0136
Employment Eligibility Verification

Please read instructions carefully before completing this form. The instructions must be available during completion of this form. **ANTI-DISCRIMINATION NOTICE.** It is illegal to discriminate against work eligible individuals. Employers CANNOT specify which document(s) they will accept from an employee. The refusal to hire an individual because of a future expiration date may also constitute illegal discrimination.

Section 1. Employee Information and Verification. To be completed and signed by employee at the time employment begins.

Print Name: Last	First	Middle Initial	Maiden Name

Address (Street Name and Number)		Apt. #	Date of Birth (month/day/year)

City	State	Zip Code	Social Security #

I am aware that federal law provides for imprisonment and/or fines for false statements or use of false documents in connection with the completion of this form.

I attest, under penalty of perjury, that I am (check one of the following):
☐ A citizen or national of the United States
☐ A Lawful Permanent Resident (Alien # A_____)
☐ An alien authorized to work until_____
(Alien # or Admission #_____)

Employee's Signature

Date (month/day/year)

Preparer and/or Translator Certification. *(To be completed and signed if Section 1 is prepared by a person other than the employee.) I attest, under penalty of perjury, that I have assisted in the completion of this form and that to the best of my knowledge the information is true and correct.*

Preparer's/Translator's Signature	Print Name

Address (Street Name and Number, City, State, Zip Code)	Date (month/day/year)

Section 2. Employer Review and Verification. To be completed and signed by employer. Examine one document from List A OR examine one document from List B **and** one from List C as listed on the reverse of this form and record the title, number, and expiration date, if any, of the document(s).

List A	OR	List B	AND	List C
Document title: _____		_____		_____
Issuing authority: _____		_____		_____
Document #: _____		_____		_____
Expiration Date (if any):_____		_____		_____
Document #: _____				
Expiration Date (if any):_____				

CERTIFICATION - I attest, under penalty of perjury, that I have examined the document(s) presented by the above-named employee, that the above-listed document(s) appear to be genuine and to relate to the employee named, that the employee began employment on (month/day/year) _____**and that to the best of my knowledge the employee is eligible to work in the United States. (State employment agencies may omit the date the employee began employment).**

Signature of Employer or Authorized Representative	Print Name	Title

Business or Organization Name	Address (Street Name and Number, City, State, Zip Code)	Date (month/day/year)

Section 3. Updating and Reverification. To be completed and signed by employer.

A. New Name (if applicable)	B. Date of rehire (month/day/year) (if applicable)

C. If employee's previous grant of work authorization has expired, provide the information below for the document that establishes current employment eligibility.

Document Title:_____   Document #: _____   Expiration Date (if any):_____

I attest, under penalty of perjury, that to the best of my knowledge, this employee is eligible to work in the United States, and if the employee presented document(s), the document(s) I have examined appear to be genuine and to relate to the individual.

Signature of Employer or Authorized Representative	Date (month/day/year)

Form I-9 (Rev. 11-21-91) N

Glossary

Alien. Any person who is not a citizen of the United States.

Beneficiary. An alien who will obtain a visa status as the result of filing a petition or application with the INS or the Department of State.

Dependants. Spouse and children of the beneficiary under age 21.

Deportation. The process of INS intervention in removing an alien from the United States.

Dual intent. Having the intent to retain a permanent residence outside the United States. while also maintaining an intent to permanently reside in the United States.

Exclusion proceedings. The judicial process where the INS is attempting to have the court determine the alien has or had no status to enter the United States.

Immigrant. An alien who has permanent resident status in the United States.

Labor certification. Certification by the Department of Labor that there are not sufficient workers who are able, willing, qualified, and available at the place of proposed employment and that such employment will not adversely affect the wages and working conditions of workers in the United States similarly employed.

Nonimmigrant. Alien coming to the United States temporarily

Petition. Document filed with the INS, DOL, or the court seeking a status or relief.

Petitioner. Person filing the INS petiton seeking the status.

Port of entry. Physical location where the alien enters the United States that is staffed by the INS.

Priority date. The filing date of a document that starts an application or petition for a particular immigrant classification. This date assigns the applicant in a numerical position to receive an immigrant visa allotted by quotas each year.

Treaty investor. A citizen of a Party who is a business person seeking to establish, develop, administer, or provide advice or key technical services to the operation of an investment to which the business person or the business person's enterprise has committed, or is in the process of committing, a substantial amount of capital in a company.

Treaty trader. A citizen of a Party who is a business person seeking to carry on substantial trade in goods or services principally between the territory of the Party of which the business person is a citizen and the territory of the Party into which entry is sought.

Visa. The document issued by the Department of State that allows entry into the United States.

References

Bonfiglio, Joel D. *Legal Issues Effecting Joint Ventures, Mergers and Acquisitions with Canadian and Mexican Business Partners Under the NAFTA*. 25 UWLA Law Review 171 (1994).

Cheetham, Janet. Application for TN Status Under NAFTA. In Janet H. Cheetham, Editor-in-Chief, *Immigration Practice and Procedure Under the North American Free Trade Agreement*. Washington, D.C.: AILA, 1995, pp. 21–37.

D'Arelli, Paul. *Entering the Construction Service Industry in Mexico: Laws Affecting Foreign Participation, NAFTA, and Other Concerns*. 7 The Transnational Lawyer 227 (1994).

Elkind, Nancy B., Editor-in-Chief. *Employer Liability Issues in Hiring Foreign Personnel*. Washington, D.C.: American Immigration Association, 1995.

Etherington, David B., and Donna Lea Hawley. *Hiring Professionals Under NAFTA*. Immigration Briefings, No. 97-2, February 1997.

Favilla-Salano, Teresa R. *Legal Mechanisms for Enforcing Labor Rights Under NAFTA*. 18 University of Hawaii Law Review 293 (1996).

Joe, Harry J. *Temporary Entry of Business Persons to the United States under the North American Free Trade Agreement*. 8 Georgetown Immigration Law Journal 391 (1994).

Kraus, Elizabeth F. *The Systemic Effects of Economic Trade Zones on Labor Migration: The North American Free Trade Agreement and the Lessons of the European Community*. 7 Georgetown Immigration Law Journal 323 (1993).

Nugent, Charles W. *A Comparison of the Right to Organize and Bargain Collectively in the United States and Mexico: NAFTA's Side Accords and Prospects for Reform*. 7 The Transnational Lawyer 197 (1994).

Rudnick, Lawrence H. Executives, Managers, and Business People Qualifying the Non-Intracorporate Transferee Business Person. In Richard D. Steel and Michael D. Patrick, Eds., *Employment-Based Immigration: New Law and New Strategies*. Washington, D.C.: AILA, 1992, pp. 117–124.

Schoonover, Martha J., and Kathleen Campbell Walker. *Immigration Provisions of the North American Free Trade Agreement*. Immigration Briefings, No. 94-3, March 1994.

Schultz, Kenneth A. An L-1A for the Executive/Manager of a Small Business, 1994–95. In *Immigration & Nationality Law Handbook*, Volume II. Washington, D.C.: AILA, 1995.

Thompson, Elizabeth A. *Temporary U.S. Entry of Canadians Under the U.S.-Canada Free Trade Agreement*. Immigration Briefings, No. 91-1, January 1991.

Understanding Immigration Under NAFTA: A Comprehensive Guide for Practitioners and Businesses. Washington, D.C.: Federal Publications, Inc., 1994.

Walker, Kathleen Campbell, Janet Holste Cheetham, David H. Paruel, and Howard D. Greenberg. Immigration Implications of the North American Free Trade Agreement, 1994–95. In *Immigration & Nationality Law Handbook*, Volume II. Washington, D.C.: AILA, 1995.

Zulkie, Paul L. Intracompany Executives and Managers Under Section 203(b)(1)(c). In Richard D. Steel and Michael D. Patrick, Eds., *Employment-Based Immigration: New Law and New Strategies*. Washington, D.C.: AILA, 1992, pp. 125–132.

Index

accountant, 55–56
adding employers, 101–111
after-sales service, 14
agriculturist, 72
airline employees, 18
animal breeder, 72
animal scientist, 72–73
apiculturist, 73
appeal, 47
architect, 56, 136
artist, 19
astronomer, 73
athletes, 17

biochemist, 74
biologist, 74
board of directors, 16
business activities, 4, 13, 84
business visitor, 4, 6, 13–21; admission procedure, 19–20; definition, 13; period of stay, 20–21; spouse and children, 21

change in job, 113
changing employers, 101–111
children, 6, 7, 21, 47, 103, 115–122
chemist, 74

citizenship, 6, 20, 83–91, 95, 99, 103, 107, 119
commercial or industrial worker, 17
computer systems analyst, 56–57
consulate, 5, 85, 90–91

dairy scientist, 75
denial, 46, 89
dentist, 67
dietitian, 67
disaster relief insurance claims adjuster, 57
discrimination, 140, 143–144, 145–146
dual intent, 5, 88, 94, 98, 106, 110, 132
duration of stay, 20, 43, 44, 85, 89, 92

economist, 57–58
ending employment, 112–114
engineer, 58, 136
entomologist, 75
epidemiologist, 75–76
essential employees, 34–35, 36
executive, 4, 5, 23, 26, 34, 38, 43, 129–132
executive capacity, 40

extension of stay, 45–46, 92–100, 119–
    120

foreign employer, 6
foreign residence, 5, 13, 23, 37
forester, 58

geneticist, 76
geochemist, 77
geologist, 76
graphic designer, 59

H-1B visa, 7
horse race employee, 17
hotel manager, 59
horticulturist, 77–78

I-9, 139–146
immigrant, 4, 53
immigrant intent. See dual intent
industrial designer, 59–60
intent to depart, 5, 37
interior designer, 60
international fairs, 18
international trade, 23
intracompany transferee, 4, 6, 38–49,
    129–132; definition, 38, 40; denial,
    46; extension, 44–46; labor disputes,
    48–49; period of stay, 44; proce-
    dure, 41–43, 47–48; qualifying em-
    ployee, 39–41; qualifying organi-
    zation, 38–39; revocation, 46–47;
    spouse and children, 47
investment, 27–30

job shops, 33

labor certification, 36, 83, 132, 133,
    135, 137, 138
labor condition, 85–86, 97, 126
labor disputes, 48–49, 86, 125–127
land surveyor, 61
landscape architect, 61
lawyer, 61–62, 136
librarian, 62–63
license, 54–55, 56, 58, 61, 67, 68, 69,
    70, 71, 84, 89, 95, 99, 103, 107,
    111

management consultant, 63
managerial capacity, 40
managers, 5, 23, 26, 34, 43
marketing, 14
mathematician, 63–64
medical doctors, 19, 69, 136
medical laboratory technologist, 67–68
meteorologist, 78
multinational executives, 129–132
musicians, 19

nonimmigrant, 4, 5, 13, 38, 53
numerical restrictions, 4, 7–9, 19
nurse, 55, 71, 85, 99, 108
nutritionist, 68

occupational therapist, 68
out of status, 102–103, 126

passport, 83, 106
permanent residence, 5, 88, 93, 98,
    105, 110, 128–138
pharmacist, 68–69
pharmacologist, 78
photographers, 18
physician. See medical doctors
physicist, 79
physiotherapist/physical therapist, 69–
    70
plant breeder, 79
port of entry, 5, 83, 103–104, 117,
    120
poultry scientist, 79–80
prevailing wage, 85
professionals, 5, 53–82, 132–138;
    definition, 53; extension of stay, 92–
    100; procedures for admission, 83–
    91
psychologist, 70

qualification, 7
qualifying employee, 39–41

range manager/range conservationist,
    64
readmission, 112–113
recreational therapist, 70–71
religious workers, 19

research and design, 14
research assistant, 64
revocation, 46–47, 90

scientific technician/technologist, 64–65
self-employed, 6, 55
servants, 16
social worker, 65
soil scientist, 80
specialist skills, 26, 34, 36
specialized knowledge, 5, 41, 43
spouse, 6, 7, 21, 47, 103, 115–122;
   divorce, 117
strikes, 125–127
sylviculturist, 65

teachers, 81, 136
technical personnel, 26
technical publications writer, 65–66
temporary entry, 5, 13, 23
termination of employment, 114
trade, 23–25

trade dependent (TD), 6, 115–122
trade shows, 13
traders and investors, 4, 6, 22–37;
   permanent residence, 128–129
transfer of professional, 114
treaty investor, 4, 6, 26–37; control,
   31–32; definition, 26; procedure, 33–
   37; risk, 27–28; substantial, 29;
   value, 29–30
treaty trader, 4, 6, 22–26, 33–37;
   employer responsibility, 25–26;
   procedure, 33–37; trade definition,
   23–25

unlawful employment, 144–145
urban planner, 66

veterinarian, 71–72
vocational counselor, 66
voluntary service programs, 16

zoologist, 80

About the Authors

DAVID ETHERINGTON, a shareholder in the Gainesville, Florida, law firm of Etherington & Chambliss, P.A., has practiced immigration law since 1990 and is a member of the American Immigration Lawyers Association (AILA). Before relocating to Florida, he maintained a law office in the Republic of China, where he provided immigration counsel to Chinese multinational companies and served on the faculty of Tunghai University in Taichung. He is a frequent speaker and writer on immigration law matters.

DONNA LEA HAWLEY is the author of a number of legal texts and articles in Canada and the United States. She has taught at Simon Fraser University and the University of Lethbridge. She earned her law degree in 1976 and a Master's degree in anthropology of law in 1985 from the University of Alberta. She is now with the law office of Etherington & Chambliss, P.A. in Gainesville, Florida.

ISBN 1-56720-130-X

9 781567 201307

EAN

90000>

HARDCOVER BAR CODE

DATE DUE